2009 Poetry Competition

I have a dream 2009
Words to change the world

Martin Luther King

John Lennon

Global Verses
Edited by Helen Davies

First published in Great Britain in 2009 by:

Young Writers
Remus House
Coltsfoot Drive
Peterborough
PE2 9JX
Telephone: 01733 890066
Website: www.youngwriters.co.uk

All Rights Reserved
Book Design by Spencer Hart & Tim Christian
© Copyright Contributors 2009
SB ISBN 978-1-84924-489-3

Foreword

'I Have a Dream 2009' is a series of poetry collections written by 11 to 18-year-olds from schools and colleges across the UK and overseas. Pupils were invited to send us their poems using the theme 'I Have a Dream'. Selected entries range from dreams they've experienced to childhood fantasies of stardom and wealth, through to inspirational poems of their dreams for a better future and of people who have influenced and inspired their lives.

The series is a snapshot of who and what inspires, influences and enthuses young adults of today. It shows an insight into their hopes, dreams and aspirations of the future and displays how their dreams are an escape from the pressures of today's modern life. Young Writers are proud to present this anthology, which is truly inspired and sure to be an inspiration to all who read it.

Contents

Abu Dhabi Indian School, United Arab Emirates
Jaai Pakale (12) 1
Maliha Mehmood Hakim (11) 2
Aaysha Samrin (15) 3
K Lakshmi Vinayan (12) 4
A F Leonard (14) 5
Kushal Mohnot (11) 6
Rashmi Menon (16) 7
Sarah Paul (15) 8
Arya Varghese (14) 9
Varun Paleli Vasudevan (11) 10
Abhey Sham Sunder (13) 11
Pratik Kamble (11) 12

American School of Bilbao, Vizcaya, Spain
Arturo Gonzalez (11) 12
Gema Sacanell Bañuelos (12) 13
Juan Ignacio Gomeza de Larrea(11) 14
Marie Mortensen (12) 15
Paula Gonzalez Gener (12) 16

Babington Community Technology College, Leicester
Kallum McTigue (13) 16
Kelly Woods (15) 17
Carla Lange (16) 18
Bhavini Krisna (13) 19
Ganesh Vailaya (12) 20
Dominik Liggins (13) 21
Lauren Pounder (13) 21

Becket School, Nottingham
Ryan Grant (14) 22

Bo'ness Academy, Bo'ness
Campbell Meikle (12) 22
Ryan Chumley (12) 23
Kirsten Millar (12) 24

Brighouse High School, Brighouse
Natalie Henry (14) 25
Daisy Mae Crossley (12) 27
Lauren Horner (13) 29
Charlotte Owens (13) 29
Kate Powell (13) 31
Alix Whitfield (14) 31
Lucy Badrock (14) 33
George Stanley (14) 33
Frances Dugdale (13) 35
Miriam Kissack (14) 35
Sophie Marsden (13) 37
Lauren Smith (13) 37
Ciara Maxwell-Whiteley (13) 38
Karina Booth (13) 39
Sam Rawling (13) 40
Alex Sumpner (13) 41
Amy Turner (14) 42
Elyse Martin (13) 43
Jared Calvert (14) 44
Leah Grange (14) 45
Georgia Rae (13) 46
Joe Thornton (14) 47
Cameron Davies (14) 48
Victoria Frankland 49
Tom Pattinson (14) 50
Lucy Kate Ioannou (13) 51
Samuel Hardcastle (14) 52
Emily Pawson (13) 52
Peter Walker (14) 53
Eleanor Savage (13) 54
Abigail Shields (13) 55
Michael Barker (14) 56
Emily Barrett (14) 56
Amelia Carter (14) 57
Hollie Mason (14) 57
Holly Thorp (13) 58
Grace Siddle (12) 58
Alexandra Gaukrodger (13) 59
Juliette Smith (13) 60

Brynteg Comprehensive School, Bridgend
Eli Cumplido (12) 60
Emily March (12) 61
Meghan Bryant (12) 62
Jordan Tunster 62
Megan Bierney (13) 63
Cory Parry (12) 63
Marcus Cheung 64
Kierra Williams 64
Nicola Casling (11) 65
Joshua Thomas 65
Charlotte Beech (12) 66
Steven Gauci (12) 66
Sara Kirk (13) 67
Emma Johnson (12) 67
Holly Tyler (12) 68
Lola Bridgeman (12) 68
Amber Dare-Edwards (11) .. 69
Rory Nicholls 69
Callum Jones (12) 70
Bronwyn Howie 70
Alys Harrop 71
Courtney Rich 71
Eve Thomas 72
Tyler Harrison (12) 72
Cerysanne Jeffrey 73
Chloe Rosser (11) 73
Jay Coombes (12) 73
Rhys Hulme 74
Michael Short 74
Luke Rees-Davies (12) 74

Cedar Mount High School, Manchester
Rhoda Oluwadunbarin (13) ... 75
Temiloluwa Daike (14) 76
Amal Nouh (14) 77
James Collantine (12) 78
Rafiq Oladujoye (13) 78
Paige Humphries (13) 79
Keeley Fogg (12) 79
Mariam Oyebanji (13) 80
Louise Baker (12) 80
Marcus Cunningham (14) 81

Cammeron Moore (13) 81
Zachary Curran (13) 82
Shaun Gleitze (13) 82
Samuel Marrett (12) 83
Aidan Rainford (14) 83
Minh Tram Phan (13) 84
Marcin Szwanka (14) 84
Aishat Siyanbola (14) 85
Vanessa Sharp (13) 86
Tinotenda Muchirawehondo (12) 86
Jubaer Alam (13) 87
Thu Ngoc Nguyen (13) 87
Al Shady Conteh 88
Rudeen Maamoo (13) 88
Matthew Cook (14) 89
Afra Martin (12) 89
Darian Ankers (12) 90

Filey Secondary School, Filey
Matthew Sean Wright (12) 90
Alex Low (13) 91
Alan Jones (12) 92
Heather Pearson (11) 93
Lucy Miller (15) 94
Charlotte Donkin (12) 95
John Oakley (13) 96
Annabel Coleman (14) 97
Tom Crookes (11) 98
Charlotte Metcalfe (12) 98

Fosse Way School, Radstock
Cameron Carpenter (12) 99
Zoë Wilding (12) 99
Georgina Hart (12) 100
Matthew Collins (14) 100

Hodge Hill Sports & Enterprise College, Birmingham
Percy Shey 101

International School of Hyderabad, Hyderabad, India
Navya Myneni (17) 102
Valmik Kumar (16) 103

Ivy Thomas Memorial School, Montevideo, Uruguay
Clementina Orte Loustau (11) 104
Mariana Viglietti Viera (11) 105
Paula Dibueno Camano (11) 106
Irina Peyrot (11) 106

James Brindley School, Birmingham
Amy Grana De La Pena (12)
& Leomi Windsor (13) 107
Garry Jack (13) 107
Luke Price (14) 108
Ashley Bridges (13) 108

Munich International School, Starnberg, Germany
Nina-Louise Dean (12) 109
Francesca Buckley (13) 110
David Winokurow (15) 111
Chase Edwards (12) 112
Nicolas Petersen-Gyöngyösi (15) 113
Raphaela Baumgartner (14) 114
Jonathan Schiess (16) 115
Nico Kerschbaumer (15) 115

Murree Christian School, Murree, Pakistan
Johanna Liljegren (14) 116
Karuna Detsch (13) 117
Mariana Chugg (13) 118
David Smith (13) 119
Elin Isaksson (14) 120
Jared Armistead (14) 121
James Barker (13) 122
YoHan Noh (13) 123
Alex Lehmann (14) 124
Joel Stock (13) 125
Naemi Lanz (13) 126
HyoJi Song (12) 126
Michael Kietzman (14) 127
Jamie Lannon (13) 128
Jordan Lunsford (13) 129
Elizabeth Wiley (14) 130
Peter Jung (15) 131

Port Moresby International School, Boroko, Papua New Guinea
Mitlam Teno (17) 132

St Francis of Assisi RC Technology College, Aldridge
Toby Duckworth (14) 133
Megan Danks (14) 135
Laura Bradley (14) 135
Joshua Wood (14) 137
Sophie Gardner 137
Shannon MacLellan 138
Georgia Blunt 139
Shannon Williamson (13) 140
Gemma Lacey (13) 141
Henry Bath (14) 142
Alex Henley (12) 143
Thomas Bannister (14) 144
Harriet Quigley (14) 145
Eve Chambers (14) 146
Cammeron Meades (14) 147
Jake Heaney (13) 148
Mei Pang (14) 149
Daniel D'Arcy (13) 150
Lucy Myatt (13) 151
Shannan Price (12) 151
Paige Meakin-Richards (13) 152
Jessica Pridey (11) 152
Phoebe Mas-Griffin (12) 153
Haydon Delaney (13) 153
Stephanie Westley (14) 154
Luke Murphy (13) 154
Paige Somers 155
Melissa Peplow (12) 155
Sophie Lowe (13) 156
Eden Beirne (13) 156
Claudia Pocrnic (12) 157
Chantelle-Rose Hodges (12) 157

St George's College, Buenos Aires, Argentina
Daniel Claudio Bach Anzolini (13) 158
Tomas Fohrig (13) 159
Santiago Giovannetti (12)
& Pedro Landin (13) 160

Justo Scherianz
& Joaquin Rabuffetti (13) 161
Francisco Bottero (12) 162
Azul Galo (12) 163
Julianna Clark (13) 164

St Louis Grammar School, Kilkeel
Erin McEvoy (14) 165

Sawtry Community College, Huntingdon
Jessica Amy Leggett (14) 166
Sam Brooks (12) 167
Phoebe Avenell (12) 168

The Castle School, Bristol
Natasha Skinner 168
Alex Haigh 169
Rachel Spencer (13) 171
Rosanna Pearce (13) 171
Tom Bedford (13) 172
Emily Craig (13) 173
Nicky Moffat 174
Luke Williams 175
Max Hitchcock (13) 175
James Cook (13) 176
Jacob Fox (13) 176
Mikki Storton & Riddell Erridge 177
Matt Roberts 177
Jonathan Witter (13) 178
Sophie Vaughan-Williams (13) 178
Archie Stenning 179

The European School, Heredia, Costa Rica
Alexandra Ridley (12) 179

The Read School, Selby
Emily Upton (12) 180
Bryony Chapman (11) 181
Molly Browne (14) 182
Nicole Hatton (12) 183
Oscar Sugden (12) 184
Megan Backhouse (12) 185
Jacob Webster (14) 186
Phoebe Simpson (12) 187

Brooklyn Kenning (11) 188
Becca Atkinson (14) 188
Sophie Thornton (11) 189
Andrew Meiklejohn (11) 189
Eden Batley & Harriet Smith (12) 190
Hannah Jolliffe (14) 190
Lydia Quartley (12) 191
Martha Veale (12) 192
Sam Kavanagh (11) 192
Hannah Wilson (14) 193
Kashi Nair (14) 193
Laura Metcalf (11) 194
Harry Campey (13) 194
Jake Stephenson (13) 195

United World College of South East Asia, Singapore
Akshay Singh Chauhan (15) 196
Surya Sridhar (16) 197

Waverley School, Birmingham
Ali Hussain (13) 197
Sana Sikander (14) 199
Faizzan Hussain (14) 200
Saira Naz (14) 201
Zara Khan (13) 202
Juma Hussain (14) 203
Ammaarah Arfan (13) 204
Farhana Ahad (14) 205

Westley Middle School, Bury St Edmunds
Jasmine Wood & Keeley Bird (13) 205
Eleanor Trent (13) 206

West Oaks School, Wetherby
Class ASC1 206

White Ash School, Oswaldtwistle
Helen Hindle (18) 207

Witton Park Business & Enterprise College, Blackburn
Sawal Mehrban (14) 207
Ebrahim Patel (12) 208
Liam Greenwood (12)
& Sam Parkinson (13) 209

Kamran Shah (13) 209
Mollie Normington (12) 210
Tom Butterfield (11) 210
Ashleigh Blades (12) 211
Ben Dodsworth & Crystal Colbert (13) ..211
Samir Ali (14) 212
Ummehanni Suleman (11) 212
Ben Eccles (12) 213

The Poems

I Have A Dream

A hundred things to express
A thousand things to suppress
For the improvement of animals and people
Or for our nature, also called Mother Earth.

Our life has so many things in it
So many illusions, so many visions
Too many to think, to many to choose
Too many complicated sections.

Mine too is a dream, our Earth to be the best
But all that hurts, what we destroy
Let the carbon float above the Earth's chest.

'Save our Earth' every person says
But I recommend follow the plants' ways
How they try to save our breath
How they struggle to prevent our death.

We destroy plants, we eat animals
Thinking there's plenty out there
We keep hunting, we keep searching
But to find them I wonder where.

It wouldn't be the same, nor would it be fun
It would just be painful without the rising sun
Just as horror it would be
For the moon covered in carbon to see.

So just close your eyes, put on a smile
Don't sleep but walk a mile
See the plight of those who suffer because of us
See our sins going surplus.

Put a stop to excess production
Notice the air is stopping its function
Reduce the uprooting of trees
Also think of those stray animals please!

Jaai Pakale (12)
Abu Dhabi Indian School, United Arab Emirates

I Have A Dream

The pain and cry of a newborn baby that enters the world
Beyond which is a smile of a mother that nature beholds
God created life to enlighten this world with power He holds
How beautifully the moon and sun shine into silver and gold
I have a dream . . . I have a dream, and I shall go for it!

Not everything alive is visible to us
Not everything visible is alive for us
From the heavens and the skies comes a sign to inspire
Of hopes and dreams that light my heart with fire
I have a dream . . . I have a dream, and I shall go for it!

Animals and plants, mountains and forests, deserts and the sea
The world looks beautiful to me from wherever I see
I know I have a duty towards this world that I have to follow
And so, I will ensure to put in my efforts towards a better tomorrow
I have a dream . . . I have a dream, and I shall go for it!

Let us not just read history, but create one of our own
Let us learn a lesson from our mistakes that we may disown
Progress need not be limited to inventing new machines
The effort of saving this planet is hidden inside our genes
I have a dream . . . I have a dream, and I shall go for it!

I know the path is difficult and far is my destination
But I also believe in working hard with determination
Truly, those for whom failure and wealth never bothers
They learn how to share pain and sorrow from others
I have a dream . . . I have a dream, and I shall go for it!

Before death could grab me away towards a new spiritual phase
With every drop of my blood I shall contribute towards a better
                                                    human race
And as they say time shall wait for no one, so shall be it
But I have a dream to fulfil and I shall surely go for it!
I have a dream . . . I have a dream, and I shall go for it!

Maliha Mehmood Hakim (11)
Abu Dhabi Indian School, United Arab Emirates

The Dove

I was walking down the street
When something fell before my feet
I bent down to see what it was
And its fall; what was the cause?

Stunned, I stood there
I could not move
To see what was lying
Before my shoe

Shocked, I picked up the wounded bird
Stained with blood
Was the maiden of peace -
The beautiful white bird

As life slowly ebbed out
From the body of the bird
From my eye, dropped a tear
And my heart was filled with fear . . .
I let out a long sigh
Did 'peace' really die?

My mind was filled with questions and questions
About nuclear bombs and explosions
Why war and no peace?
Can't man ever live in ease?

All these questions filled my mind
It reminded me about the cruel nature of mankind
But what could I do?
And against whom?

For the world
I could only worry
And for the bird
Feel sorry.

Aaysha Samrin (15)
Abu Dhabi Indian School, United Arab Emirates

Life

Just turn around and look at what surrounds

Look at the waves and let a smile form on your face
Come and feel the breeze and let everything be at ease

Look at the moon and let him grant you a boon
Let the moonlight guide you through the darkness of the night
Let everything seem alright

Choose the path to your destiny, whether real or fantasy
Let the stars shine above you but let their light burn within you

Enjoy the beauty of Nature and let her be your teacher
Look at the mountain high and think that you could fly

Look at the trees standing still and high
Search for where the place called Paradise lies

Look for the flowers that blossom in every season
To laugh don't look for a special reason

Don't be like a volcano that erupts
Don't be like a patient who is still taking his syrups

Feel alive
Be full of life

Visit every kind of place
Be an alien from outer space

Feel the wind, hear its sound
Feel as though a new person in you has been found

Life isn't always perfect
Sad things you must forget

And move on with the rhythm of life
And live it the way it's like

For that as you know is life!

K Lakshmi Vinayan (12)
Abu Dhabi Indian School, United Arab Emirates

We Still Dream On

In my deep, dark memories
Where no one's eyes can see
Firing ideas never cease
Of what I want the world to be.

We never notice this wonderful power
Even when on us catastrophes dawn
Imagination blooms like a flower
And yes, we still dream on.

If I had the wealth and gold
To rule the land and sea
I'd give it all to young and old
And abolish poverty.

Then from the highest steeple
I'll call out across the seas
And ask all my people
To get me one of these:

One who turns the unforgiving foe
Into a faithful friend
A man who shall never feel woe
Until his very end.

A place where peace always prevails
A Heaven on this Earth
Where friendship never fails
And enmity is dirt.

That's why we never fear
Even when on us catastrophes dawn
As long as we're here
We still dream on . . .

A F Leonard (14)
Abu Dhabi Indian School, United Arab Emirates

The Fire Of My Will To Change

Even if I were the last man on Earth
I would change, for sure I would
From Moscow to Cairo, from Tokyo to Perth
To change, for sure I would.

If in a crowd of millions, supporting
A cause for good
A reason to support justice
I would change, for sure I would.

With integrity, belief and faith
Trust, truth and no more hate
We could break mountains; we could break the sky
And all this I promise to you mate.

I will change with impact, with power
With one simple idea
To revolutionise the world
But I would need you and only you.

I'd walk through snow in search of heat
I'd fly to Pluto in search of light
I'd do anything which would
Change the minds of millions.

To make a difference if I had a choice
I would prefer education
'Cause if I had to innovate I'd do it the way
That creates satisfaction.

I promise, through any way, sure any way
I would turn the world, the world upside down
Through any manner
I would revolutionise.

Kushal Mohnot (11)
Abu Dhabi Indian School, United Arab Emirates

I Have A Dream

I have a dream
It shines in the dark as bright as a sun
Will never dry up like a mirage in the desert

I have a dream
It has no end
Nor any start
But a life within

I have a dream
Many voiced for it
Many fought for it
And much happened
But that much was very little

I have a dream
Many promised - take a step and we are there
But, it was only metaphorically

I have a dream
To make it a reality
To see the days of glory of human race
And human rights through me

I have a dream
No mountain is so high
No sea is so deep
It carries my dreams of many round the world
For it I will give my all

I have a dream
To see a world
With no answer to questions of nationality, caste, religion
But only one answer - *'We are humans.'*

Rashmi Menon (16)
Abu Dhabi Indian School, United Arab Emirates

I Have A Dream

I have lots of dreams but
The most wonderful dream
Is of my motherland, India
The land of my dreams
A place where everyone loves to be
A place where everyone is equal
A place where the sweet fragrance of flowers
Is smelt against the fresh smell of woods
This land is magnificent to see
Greenery everywhere, fills the eye with joy
A place which is alien to the sounds of distant
War cry and clash of swords
A place where there is the mightiest clash of words
This land is free from mighty headed dragon-terrorism
A land where we follow the principles of secularism
Here everyone is educated, everyone is free
Where everyone has his daily bread
Where everyone can work without threat
This place is a poet's delight, a pilgrim's soul
An artistic masterpiece, a dream of all
A land where the dazzling white flag flutters high
A place where pen is indeed mightier than the sword
A country above all the rest
The mightiest power in Asia, a heaven for tourists
The choice of investors, a light in darkness
In this land there isn't a spell we can't reverse
No curse we can't break, nor
Any evil we can't oppose
But this is just a dream, which you and I could make true
My dream of a magnificent India.

Sarah Paul (15)
Abu Dhabi Indian School, United Arab Emirates

All Shall Pass Away

I had a treasure which I prized
Whose touch healed broken minds
But in a little spark of the day
It had all passed away.

In just a little spark
Of kindness when the day is dark
My thoughts, feelings, everything I knew
It had all passed away.

Though nonchalant and eminent was I
Enigmatic and ebullient
All the joy, goodness and greatness I possessed
It had all passed away.

Estranged by all, ennui filled
Oblivious was I to all I've done right
I walked lonely, I lost everything
Like the last leaf to fall.

All my laughter gone
I walked pale and gaunt
Lonely steps I walked
With no one to guide or help.

Life is brutal, scary and dark
It's always filled with pain and anguish
But like all good days once possessed
These days too will pass someday.

Arya Varghese (14)
Abu Dhabi Indian School, United Arab Emirates

A Dream

A dream or an ambition,
Whatever it may be.
A lawyer or a pilot,
Anything will do for me.

I can rule the skies,
Or fly with the rules.
I may not be both,
And can be something else too.
But I certainly have the will
To do my best.
I shall work very hard,
And then have my rest.

Life is a mystery,
With hidden hints behind.
Where will it lead me?
The answer is from the Divine.

A dream or an ambition,
Whatever it may be.
A lawyer or a pilot,
Anything will do for me.

Varun Paleli Vasudevan (11)
Abu Dhabi Indian School, United Arab Emirates

My Dream For A Better Future

In a million, I am only one
But for a better future, I have a dream
It is not related to personal gain or fun
As all the other dreams may seem
Changing the world, my dream is about
And ending every evil practice
This dream coming true, I truly doubt
But then who will enjoy a world of peace?
The modern generation's influence
Has spoilt the humanity
The humans are left with no moral sense
Of at least greeting with hospitality
To end today's corruption
Is my aim to achieve
A better world's creation
Is what I want to perceive
Will my dreams come true?
For a better and brighter tomorrow
I really hope they do
For our peace with no more sorrow!

Abhey Sham Sunder (13)
Abu Dhabi Indian School, United Arab Emirates

Save Mother Earth

I have a dream
Of a world filled with esteem
I would help the needy
Who linger in the city
For the people I know
They have to believe
That the world is dying
And we're just sighing
So keep your city clean
Before the Earth starts begging, please
Save Mother Earth
By not littering
And fulfil my dream
Before we sleep.

Pratik Kamble (11)
Abu Dhabi Indian School, United Arab Emirates

Emerald Turtle

I saw an emerald turtle
Swimming in the river
Trying to escape
From that mortal place

Why are so many factories
Beside the rivers?

Wouldn't it be better to see
Seventy emerald turtles?

Arturo Gonzalez (11)
American School of Bilbao, Vizcaya, Spain

Pollution

We live in a world
Full of dirt and contamination
The air and water we drink is polluted
Everything is polluted

When you go to the beach
And throw something to the floor
You're polluting

Maybe you'll think:
It's just a little piece of paper
What harm can it do?
Well it can do a lot of harm
And, what if everybody thinks that way?
Then everybody would throw a little piece of trash
That adds to all the rest

A lot of animals and plants are dying
Because of us
Even Earth is dying
Just because of us

We destroy woods and fields
To make houses or roads
But we don't think
That that is someone's home

Help to stop this
Help save your planet
And everything on it
Including
You.

Gema Sacanell Bañuelos (12)
American School of Bilbao, Vizcaya, Spain

Babies

I have a dream
That children can live
So many things can happen
To those fragile creatures
They can die
When they have their first sight

Crying for all reasons
So beautiful
But for some reason
Their parents abandon them, in the streets

Sometimes you can hear their little hearts
Pumping as fast as I can run
And then it's all silence -
No more cries
But a little body
So still
Without
L
I
F
E.

Juan Ignacio Gomeza de Larrea(11)
American School of Bilbao, Vizcaya, Spain

Abandoned Animals

One of the things
I really don't like
Is an animal left in pain

It's not like a teddy
It's not like a doll
It is someone who can't complain

A starving horse
A dog on a chain . . .
I've seen it happen, haven't you?

When I see those things
My heart grows cold
And the sky is no longer blue

How good for me
That volunteers help
Their time on pets they spend

So this is how my poem will end:
That's the way to treat a friend!

Marie Mortensen (12)
American School of Bilbao, Vizcaya, Spain

Change The World

I'm a person who wants peace
Like few people I don't follow the sheep
Excuse me if I'm outspoken
But I have to speak
If not, who will?
The world is for everyone
To be together and happy
Not for wars and fights
But human rights.

We're all humans
Believe it or not
Your inside is what matters and makes you special
Not the colour of your skin
Whether you are black or white
We all have the right
To be what we want
And to be . . .
Free.

Paula Gonzalez Gener (12)
American School of Bilbao, Vizcaya, Spain

I Have A Dream

I have a dream
I have a dream
For racism and terrorism
To go away, away for good
Chuck them out of the window
Don't give them a yellow card
Give racism the red card
Do you
Like racism? I don't
Shall we put them in the bin and lock
It up forever?

Kallum McTigue (13)
Babington Community Technology College, Leicester

Not A Butterfly, Not A Canary

Watching the rooftops
Observing the street
Finding where the rainbow stops
Never, ever using my feet.

Laughter resounds
From an emerald-green garden
No children to be found
Just a lot of beer-fueled men.

Smiling to myself
I take flight higher into the clouds
Perch upon one like a shelf
Bask in the sun that's shining now.

Squawks overhead
Of passing swans and geese
I can't help but dread
The 'gifts' they might release.

Before they have the chance
I rise and fall gracefully
Tumbling to the ground in a dance
Make sure no one sees me.

All too soon it's time to return home
Camera in hand I start to run
Hear the high-pitched squeal of my phone
Finally I wake to the glare of the sun.

Kelly Woods (15)
Babington Community Technology College, Leicester

Land In The Stars

See a dream that seems too distant
And some people just won't try
They give up without fighting for it
And eventually it dies

But I can't live that kind of lifestyle
I need something to hope for
I never stop hoping opportunity
Will knock upon my door

'Cause even if it takes forever
And my progress seems so slow
I remember that an oak tree
Takes it own sweet time to grow

And I know that any life
Without a dream is dark and dull
And I could never live with that

I know any hope is worth having
No matter how far out it seems
Cause everyone gets fifteen minutes
Where they can live their dream

So if it seems unlikely
I'll shoot for space, and Mars
Cause even if I miss the moon
I'll land on the stars.

Carla Lange (16)
Babington Community Technology College, Leicester

One Day It Came, One Day It Went

Pain and crying, all left in grief
Scars it made, it hides behind
Still shows the stain with dreary face.

Friends they were, both kith and kin
All lost, eyes all filled
Painted red were streets and straights
All tell the tale of grizzly deeds.

Distress. Anger and fear around
Shaken we were, all in one go
Hand in hand, let's stand behind
With martyrs, they gave it all.

Shoulders we gave for heads to cry
For sure we knew that all were one
Arms wide stretched and open hearts
Stood all true in words and deeds.

Time has come for us to rise
Time to prove that we won't fail
With pride atop let's hold arms tight
It's time to shine and see all fine.

Bhavini Krisna (13)
Babington Community Technology College, Leicester

I Have A Dream

I have a dream to win the war against drugs
To be free of that intoxicating poison
I have a dream to banish poverty
Everyone equal and healthy
I have a dream to make the environment safe
Nature growing to be vibrant and strong
I have a dream to unite the countries
East, West, North, South, all in harmony.

All children have a right to be educated
They have a right to have fun
They have a right to mould their own lives
They have a right to shine.

All animals deserve to live
To roam their habitat safe from harm
They have the right to live the way they want
They are equal to Man
They do not deserve to be captured and tortured.

I have a dream
Every organism is a light. Every organism is hope . . .

Ganesh Vailaya (12)
Babington Community Technology College, Leicester

My Dreams

I have a dream to stop the wars
To help people on drugs.

I have a dream
To be a footballer
But I want to stop people destroying the world.

I have a dream
I dream to be a runner
But I want to help old people.

I have lots of dreams
But I don't know what to do
I hope I can do them all
It's going to be hard.

Dominik Liggins (13)
Babington Community Technology College, Leicester

I Wish I Could

I wish I could help
The children in Pakistan
Because of the pain they are in.

I wish I could
Stop racism
Because it hurts my feelings.

I wish I could
Stop people who disrespect other people's religions.

I wish I could
Make people respect others
And make the world a better place.

Lauren Pounder (13)
Babington Community Technology College, Leicester

Hoping

When husbands go to war the family are hoping that they come back alive!
They hope they don't see a car pulling up outside the house
and a sergeant coming to say, 'Sorry, but he's gone.'
And then if they don't get letters home just saying, 'How are you' or 'I'm missing you'
The family stops hoping that in a couple of weeks they'll be coming
back home because thoughts are flying through their minds.

But if all wars stop, families won't be hoping that no car will pull up outside
and hoping that he will come back alive!

Ryan Grant (14)
Becket School, Nottingham

I Have A Dream

I have a dream and I have a plan
To be a marine biologist - if I can
To dive down in the deep, blue sea
Is definitely the best place for me
To swim among the sharks and fishes
Is one of the greatest of my wishes
To discover a new species down below
Which only me and the creature would know
It is my very strong belief
That Man must act to save the reef
The population must do better
Or one day we'll all be wetter
Across the lands and pole to pole
And in the ozone where there's a hole
In places endangered is where I'll be
So I can help save our land and sea
And all the animals and the trees
From the biggest whale to the littlest bees
All these beings deserve a life
Not to be destroyed by Man (and his wife!)

Campbell Meikle (12)
Bo'ness Academy, Bo'ness

I Have A Dream

I have a dream
A wonderful one at that
So, you wish to hear?
Well, let's have a chat.

In my dream
I can fly
And people do not fight
Time goes by
So very, very quickly.

In my dream
Wars don't exist
Skin colour doesn't matter
Who cares if we're black or white?
Or who is thin or who is fatter?
All of *this* I don't understand
We all have a right
All God's brand!

In my dream
Everything's fun!
I can play until my heart's content
Underneath the blazing sun
I have many friends here
All of whom I wish were real.

But when my dream world gets covered by night
It's morning in reality
All of this that I wished was real
Will always be something only *I* feel . . .

Ryan Chumley (12)
Bo'ness Academy, Bo'ness

I Have A Dream

I've had a dream
We all wore masks
Behind which we did hide
Concealing from the world
Who we truly were inside.

Afraid to show our faces
Like the sun behind a cloud
Hiding individuality
Of which we should be proud.

If we all removed our masks
And showed our different faces
Different hearts, different minds
Different shapes and different races.

The world would be a better place
If we could only realise
We are all here for a purpose
And see through each other's eyes.

I have a dream
Where every person
Can be their person
And be remembered
For who they are
Not for the mask they wore,

Kirsten Millar (12)
Bo'ness Academy, Bo'ness

Sleep

Close you eyes
Don't cry, it's over now
Fourteen years of pain can be forgotten
Now sleep my child
You'll never have to wake again.

Just sleep.

You'll be remembered as you always were
The sun that shone
Even when the clouds were grey
And your warmth could heat a room
Even on the coldest day
But your mind was dark and cold
You couldn't chase the pain away.

Just sleep.

You could make a stranger love you
You were so happy
What in your life went wrong?
Your life could have been compared
To a happy song
But without a middle
Just a beginning and an end.

Just sleep.

Now I must say goodbye forever
One thing left to say
Why did you not tell me
The pain you felt inside?
What was wrong? I could not see
I never said goodbye
I could have saved your life.

It's over now.

Just
Sleep.

Natalie Henry (14)
Brighouse High School, Brighouse

The Key To My Heart

I've been given a key
To a special place
I got it when I was born
Along with my hands and face

It has never left my conscience
It has never left my mind
For it is something special
That I am going to find

You wonder where my key is
But you can never see
I don't wonder why you wonder
For it is inside of me

My key doesn't go in a keyhole
My key can't open a door
I have never even seen my key
But I experience it more and more

The key is a feeling
Everyone has, like me
For my key is hope
It's not really a key

It slowly opens a door
To a world of peace and freedom
That's why it is a key
It tells what needs to be done

Hope is like energy
A positive powerful wish
It burns like a core inside of you
It is something we fail to miss

Do not fail to listen
To this powerful thought
For you can make it happen
Just do what you've been taught

If there is hope there is an answer
Waiting to be found
Hope doesn't appear for any reason
It means there is a solution around

One day you may struggle
Something is hard to face
But hope is always there
To help you to the surface

Hope is like instructions
Of things we all want done
So when I consult my key
Why are things not fun?

The things that spring to mind
When I think about my hopes
Are people who need help
People who can't cope

They have a right to peace
And they all have their faith and dreams
Running through them like a river
Or even trickling like a stream

Hope is a powerful thing
It engages my heart
Leads my brain the right way
Tells me where to start

A small stone can make a splash
A cloud becomes a storm
So a person can produce miracles
In any shape or form.

Daisy Mae Crossley (12)
Brighouse High School, Brighouse

I Have A Dream

I have a dream
A dream of peace
Of love and equality
A poppy wreath

I have a dream
A dream of power
Of no hurt and racism
Hour by hour

I have a dream
A dream of freedom
Of no murder and war
In each kingdom

I have a dream
A dream of hope
Of truth and no shame
It's been blessed by the Pope

I have a dream
A dream of no hell
Of no sins and mistakes
No reason to yell

I have a dream
A dream of laughter
Of right and no wrong
A happy ever after

I have a dream
A dream of no pain
Of free will and no lies
Again and again

I have a dream
A dream of respect
Of no bullies and thugs
No need to protect

I have a dream
A dream of kindness
Of sharing and giving

No deafness and blindness

I have a dream
A dream of belief
Of no heartbreak and sorrow
Enough pain relief

I have a dream
A dream of no crime
Of no drugs and drunk people
No need to steal dimes.

Lauren Horner (13)
Brighouse High School, Brighouse

The Death Penalty

Worry
And torture
Sat in a cell
Beads of sweat run
Down their faces. Wondering
And hoping, all alone. Will
They live to see another day?
Innocent men awaiting their fate
Wishing they could see their child
Again. Stood in silence praying: praying
For a miracle. Mind racing, room spinning
Hands shaking, heart pounding, *why me?*
Why this? Why today? Why ever? Innocent
Women walk across the cold corridor
Then down the hall to reach their
Destiny. Take their last few steps
Into their final room, breathing
Their last ever breath - leaving
For Heaven. Yet another
Falsely accused victim
Of the death
Penalty.

Charlotte Owens (13)
Brighouse High School, Brighouse

The Times: What A Wonderful World
(Inspired by the song 'What A Wonderful World' by Louis Armstrong)

Page 1
Army Pounds Taliban

I see skies of grey
Dead roses too
And I think to myself
What a wonderful world?

Page 2
Kidnap Victim Is Found
Bound And Gagged With
Bomb strapped To His
Belly

I see skies of grey
Dead roses too
And I think to myself
What a wonderful world?

Page 3
Al-Qaeda Threat To Kill
British Hostage

I see skies of grey
Dead roses too
And I think to myself
What a wonderful world?

Page 4
Second Body Found
After Brother And
Sister Lost In Flood

I see skies of grey
Dead roses too
And I think to myself
What a wonderful world?

Page 5
Burnt, Broken, Silent;
The Child Victims Of
Tamil War

I see skies of grey
Dead roses too
And I think to myself
What a wonderful world?

Kate Powell (13)
Brighouse High School, Brighouse

Those Numbers

Her world is full of darkness
Her life has no hope
Every day brings new struggles
How is she to cope?

Her father beats her
Her mother swears
Her sisters laugh
For her no one cares.

She sees the phone
Dials the number
999 in her head
She knows she can stop this.

The door breaks down
The windows smash
Through come the police
Responsible for this clash.

Out they go
Both through the door
In her world
Pain exists no more.

Her life has new hope
She breathes fresh air
Those numbers - 999
Have saved her life.

Alix Whitfield (14)
Brighouse High School, Brighouse

Hope For A Smile

The corner of my bedroom
I sit on the cold floor
The clouds begin to loom
And I hear my daddy roar

I try to find someone to cling on
I try to find a shoulder to cry on
What did I ever do wrong?
Why should I feel in the wrong?

My bruises ache, I'm full of pain
My body's full of fear
I know it's starting all over again
As I sense my daddy's near

What did I ever do wrong?
Why should I feel in the wrong?

I sit and wait, what else was there left to do?
I look through the window for a guiding light
When I see the family next door, their smiles shining through
Everything 'fit' their happiness feels so right

What did I ever do wrong?
Why should I feel in the wrong?

I notice the pictures on the wall
Everything looks so right
I know I can run without having to fall
Run to a future like my colourings, bright

The light through the window, the guiding smiles
Everything let me know I should run
I could run and run for a hundred miles
And all this pain and anxiety could be done

What did I ever do wrong?
Why should I feel in the wrong?

I grab my teddy, then my feet take me away
Never stop running, just keep going
I need to leave, make daddy pay
My tears roll, my every emotion showing

The thought of those families' smiles
Make those blisters all worthwhile.

Walking, jogging, running, running, running . . .

Lucy Badrock (14)
Brighouse High School, Brighouse

A Dream

I was born with a dream
A target, a goal
I wanted to visit stars, planets
And see a black hole.

I laid there in bed
Every moonlit night
Looking through my window
At the stars so bright.

One night I saw a shooting star
I wished
I begged
Someday I would travel that far.

I laid there again, day after day
Still nothing came so I started to pray
Finally a star came through the night so blue
Once again I wished my dream would come true.

I worked my way through school, with the same dream
Things got harder, well that's how they seemed
Kids said I had no chance, that my dream was a dud
But deep down inside me I knew that I could.

I knew I would show them, and do it someday
I would be flying so fast through the Milky Way
I cleared my throat with a cough
I closed my eyes and 3, 2, 1, blast off!

George Stanley (14)
Brighouse High School, Brighouse

Undecided

I have a dream that one day
The world will be full
The world will be free
The world will be happy
Just like me

But am I truly happy
Or is my life just a fake?
As fake as the romances in the movies
Or the reasoning that they take?

Yes I have a good life
I have money, I have prospects
I have a future
Or do I?

Could my life be a lie?
I walk down the street
People always like me
Or do they?

Do people really like me?
Or do I just think they do?
So clouded by the fog in my head
I can't see what's surely true

I get up in the morning
Put on my make-up and hair extensions
Too scared of what people will think
If I don't

Is it so wrong just to be me?
Will my friends still be my friends?
With or without the make-up?
Am I really that different?

So many insecurities
Stuck in my own little world
But what about the world outside my own?
Should I take a step outside my own front door?

I found something bigger than all of us out there
Something that comes from the soul

It broke through the life I used to lead
And found the bravery I'd always had.

The bravery to change.

Frances Dugdale (13)
Brighouse High School, Brighouse

Colours Of The Future

The future is a kaleidoscope
You gaze through from space
The image starts fading
The picture starts changing

The pink of the blossom
The white for the cold
The green of the summer
The harvest that's gold

The image is fading
The picture is changing

The blackening cloud
The brown of the wood
The crowd full of colours
The red for the blood

The image is fading
The picture is changing

Red for the fire
Brown for the mud
Grey of the famine
Blue of the flood

The picture has changed
The image has faded
And now it has gone.

Miriam Kissack (14)
Brighouse High School, Brighouse

Dreams

We all have dreams
And ambitions alike
Even if you don't notice
They are waiting for you to strike

You might want to change the world
If you try it might happen one day
If at first you don't succeed
Just try another way

It might be to stop cruelty to children
For this you should strive
Because if you believe in and follow this dream
In happiness they will thrive

It might be to stop bullies
Stop people being picked on
If you keep working towards this dream
You can make people's sadness be gone

It might be to help people worse off
Who might be living rough
If you try to achieve this dream
Their lives might not be so tough

You wonder why other people can't see
The dreams that make you
But they can't strike the dreams like you can
These dreams that are you through and through

These dreams need not be struck
Like a pot of gold
They might not be perfect yet
But they are there for you to mould

Find those dreams so that they are there
Close enough to hold
They could brighten up your life
So make them big and bold

So don't make other people
Find a code or key
Show them what you're all about
This is the real me.

Sophie Marsden (13)
Brighouse High School, Brighouse

You Can Do It

Drugs, abuse, alcohol
Imagine waking up sweating
Desperate for your next hit
Imagine waking up to find your
Father attacking your mother
Imagine waking up sweating
Desperate for your next drink
Drugs, abuse, alcohol.

Drugs, abuse, alcohol
Getting past this may seem
Impossible
It's challenging, complicated and
Hard
But you can do it
If you try, you can do it
Drugs, abuse, alcohol.

Freedom, happiness, joy
Imagine waking up alcohol free
Imagine waking up to find a
Happy family
Imagine waking up clean
Freedom, happiness, joy.

You should run your own life
Don't let anyone or anything get in the way.

Lauren Smith (13)
Brighouse High School, Brighouse

Words Make History

How can one person change the world?
To me it still remains a mystery
Inner strength, patience and honesty,
The words they say, making history.

To get all the people together
And the truth to be finally told,
Nothing can ever buy freedom;
Not silver, diamonds or gold.

It all starts with a dream,
Of which they can only pray,
That God will see their suffering
And help them on their way.

As the protests cause an uproar,
Mothers calling for help as their babies cry,
The forces begin to wage war
From which many innocent people die.

A dream can inspire millions:
One voice in the crowd will be listened to.
They can influence the future,
Change the world, so dreams can come true.

They help guide the way,
The bright light breaking the everlasting dark,
By defying the rules of others,
On history they make a mark.

Some say actions speak louder than words,
But the words must inspire more,
From mixing religions and races
To completely rewriting law.

So what has the world come to?
Into this terror we have been hurled,
To better it for all the people
A few small words can change the world.

Ciara Maxwell-Whiteley (13)
Brighouse High School, Brighouse

The Future

Roses are red
Violets are blue
I love this world
I hope you do too

The sun is bright
The grass is green
The meadows shimmer
The countryside's serene

This world may soon be gone
If we do not stop
Within the blink of an eye
We may all get a shock

The ice caps are melting
The rainforests are going
The temperature's rising
The dust bowls are blowing

Polar bears are dying
Animals losing their homes
Food chains being cut off
Leave their habitats alone

But we as humans
Are responsible for all this
All the global warming
The poisonous oil rigs

So the future of the world
Depends on all of us
So stop travelling by cars and planes
And please travel by bus

So roses are red
Violets are blue
So leave it that way
And save the world too!

Karina Booth (13)
Brighouse High School, Brighouse

Why War?

Living in an undersized mud hut
Walking miles in only bare foot
Searching for water
Being shot by a mortar
But what is next to come?

You're missing your wife
Only armed with a knife
The Afghan soldiers
Draw guns from their holders
And threaten to shoot you down
But what is next to come?

Why should they suffer
From a prime mistake?
Why should they suffer
For goodness sake?
Why should they suffer
Scared to live their life?

Being proud to be alive
Next thing being shot to the ground
How can you think this is fair?

The war must stop
And it must stop *now*
What has the community done?

Terror, madness, sadness, weak, afraid, alone

Think this is fair?
The answer is *no*

Stop death
Stop terror
Stop sadness
Stop war
Full stop.

Sam Rawling (13)
Brighouse High School, Brighouse

The Flames

I awoke to the strong smell of smoke
The sharp burning flames burst up around me
Every time I turned, my back began to burn
And all around me I could see
All the folk looking at me
All shaking their heads in disbelief

The creaking floor gave me a sign
That she was still alive
I had to help; I had to save, but how?
And all around me I could see
All the folk looking at me
All shaking their heads with disbelief
All thinking the same thing

I picked her up from the floor
She did not move at all
The silence shivered down my spine
As all her memories she would leave behind
And all around me I could see
All the folk looking at me
All shaking their heads in disbelief
All thinking the same thing
How could this have happened?

I hugged the body with all my love
I let her leave in peace
I sat on the floor and started to cry
It was time for her to leave me
And all around me I could see
All the faces of misery
Suddenly I see the truth
The truth that'll haunt me forever
I forgot to put it out

I killed my daughter.

Alex Sumpner (13)
Brighouse High School, Brighouse

To Write Love On Your Arms

Imagination thrives on inner want
Building dreams from subconscious thought
Dreams of survival and saviour
When one of those dreams come true
It gives others hope of the same

'Tell them to look up
Tell them to remember the stars'
That's what she said that night
For all the pain she still cares
She fought on through and she's here today.

The people in our lives are not just bodies
They're not to make a number
They're there to help and to save
Not just family, but friends
The people who stay when others walk away.

'The stars are always there
But we miss them in the dirt and cloud
We miss them in the storms
Tell them to remember hope. We have hope'
She knew she would survive.

When she was found, cocaine was devouring her
She hadn't slept in days
Her nineteen years hid in bandages
But she was strong, and she's here
She's living proof dreams come true.

She gave up the razor and found love
She would ask you to remember
She'd want you to carry on breathing
To think before you decided it was enough
Because there's always someone behind you.

Willing to catch you.

Amy Turner (14)
Brighouse High School, Brighouse

Holding On

You were the reason that I woke up in the morning
You were the reason that I went to sleep at night
You were the reason that I wondered
If there was love at first sight

You were worth every bone in my body
Every beat in my heart
To know that we would always be together
To know that we would never be apart

But then one day it all changed
My whole world fell apart
Who knew that one simple noise
Could clearly break your heart

Gunshot fire surrounded me
A gut wrenching cry of sorrow
He knew that my heart was broken
Because for him there was no tomorrow

The pit of my stomach felt empty
My heart had been shattered like glass
To know that my true love forever
Would be buried under the grass

I cried at that moment for years
Until someone reached out a hand
He wiped away the tear from my eye
Suddenly my heart became whole
All at his command

You may not understand the pain
You may have completely lost track
But the moral of this poem is
Do not hold on to the past.

Elyse Martin (13)
Brighouse High School, Brighouse

In The Future

Today is just another day

Tomorrow will be just like today
No advances made, nothing interesting happened

In a week something will have happened
Be it a major disaster or improvement
Or something in your personal life

In a month lots will have happened
To you and the world
Death and life
Joyful and sad

In a year we look back
On what's previously passed
Thinking of people we have lost
Things we have gained
And what's to come

In a decade we will have
Amazingly awesome androids
Electric cars saving the Earth
Hope of no war
Hope of no sickness
Hope of more money

In the future
The world will be better
A better world
Better people
Better place
Or will it all just be the same?

Everything just like today?

Jared Calvert (14)
Brighouse High School, Brighouse

Road To Recovery

You've been through so much
But you're still so strong
I know you'll get through this
I knew all along
Day by day
You become so much stronger
And you know the pain
Won't last much longer.

Though times got tough
You still had hope
People were amazed
How well you coped
Your smile fills the room
Your heart warms the cold
We all know you'll be here
'Till you're grey and old.

Through thick and thin
Through day and night
You're on the road to recovery
I can see the light!
You really made me realise
Life is worth living
And at every chance
Take what you're given.

Leah Grange (14)
Brighouse High School, Brighouse

My 'Best One'

I think of you throughout the bad times
I see you and see the sun
I see a star and think of you
My only friend, my 'best one'.

But then I see you, your smiling eyes
Gazing at me
And you make me go on
Whatever life brings us we're always
Going strong.

You're a role model to me
Whenever I see you I never want to leave
You do everything for me and still
Make me believe.

So different, yet so close
You could say I'm everything you're not
You could say I follow you I suppose
Still after all, we've been through quite a lot.

Ok, we're friends but yes we are family
You inspire me to live life to its best
Through every slip and every test
I could thank you yet that might sound sad
But without you, well, I think I'd
Go mad!

Georgia Rae (13)
Brighouse High School, Brighouse

My Dream

I dream that I could go to school
To learn lots of stuff
The lessons would be really cool
But it might be quite tough
I'd still help my family out on our farm herding cattle
But to get a good job I would have to battle
I'm an African boy

I dream of a world without war
One that is full of peace
I wouldn't be scared any more
If the firing ceased
I'd still worry when I saw a British soldier with a gun
But at least I'd know his job was done
I'm an Iranian girl

I dream of the new shooting game
When I've completed it
By making the enemy lame
Without having to quit
I dream for the school holidays
When I won't learn maths
And won't have homework each day
So I'll play Combat Clash
I'm a British boy.

Joe Thornton (14)
Brighouse High School, Brighouse

I Dream

I dream long and hard
About what the world will be in 2033.

I dream of flying saucers
Good or bad, who knows
I dream of aliens
From near and far
I have a dream.

I dream of moving robots
To care for my every need
I dream of smaller phones
Small enough to fill a pocket
I have a dream.

I dream of no drugs, alcohol and smoking
So everyone lives healthily
I dream of no depression or recession
To keep the Earth going strong
I have a dream.

But I leave this dream
Because I have to live in the present
But I can still dream.

Cameron Davies (14)
Brighouse High School, Brighouse

Too Weak To Fight

The night is so dark, so harsh, and so cold
Was this our only warning?
The fragile friendships
We now hold
Will they still be here in the
Morning?

His steel capped boots echo
Loud like his hate
His gun lingers, lifeless
At his side
Only this Nazi can decide
Our fate
Lying shivering in
Bed we have nowhere
To hide.

Bang!
And then he is gone
With hundreds more dead tonight
This catastrophe has been going on too long
But we are all too weak to fight!

Victoria Frankland
Brighouse High School, Brighouse

Anger Throughout

The anger came through
As the door was slammed in my face
I shut my eyes just in case
I clenched my fists hard
Then looked over the derelict yard
The trees blew hard in the wailing wind
And as I watched I felt like I had sinned.

My eyes were watering
My mouth was dry
Then I felt like I was going to die
The penny dropped
But somehow I didn't know the reason
At this terrible time in the season.

Bang! Why did it happen to her?
'What did you see sir?'
The policemen asked
'Do you know who did this to her?'
This made me put myself under the knife
And this for all the anger throughout my life.

Tom Pattinson (14)
Brighouse High School, Brighouse

Child Abuse

Sat in the dark
Wondering what you did wrong
And why this had to happen to you
Hoping one day, things will change
Wondering when your life became
So tragic and frightening
And knowing it'll never be the same again
Thinking about what it felt to be loved
And not treated so bad
That you're afraid to breathe
You remember when you lied
To everyone every single day, about when
You 'walked into the door again'
Or 'fell down the stairs'
And constantly hiding your scars
That will remain with you for the rest of your life
On the inside, and the out.

Child abuse
Let's put a *stop* to it.

Lucy Kate Ioannou (13)
Brighouse High School, Brighouse

Chances

When you have a dream
Something you want to do
Live life how you want to
Live it to the full.

If you want to be
A doctor, vet or nurse
If you work hard enough
It could just be for you.

Or if you want to be
In a job of any kind
A bit of dedication
You'll have it in no time.

So whatever you want to do
You always have a chance
So live life to the full
Live life to the max!

Samuel Hardcastle (14)
Brighouse High School, Brighouse

Seasons

I stand there tall, bold and strong
People say I'm weak, but I know they're wrong.

I shelter young faces away from the rain
Each day I see their forever growing pain

Secretly listening to each conversation
I watch you close with awe and admiration

Children are playing all around
All around my feet as I clutch to the ground

In the autumn, half of me disappears
Until they return later the next year.

Emily Pawson (13)
Brighouse High School, Brighouse

The Luke Of My Life

The sun that shines through the clouds
He is the calf in a herd of cows
He is the one I strive to be
He is my Luke Baranyai.

He protects his family in times of trouble
He is so nice and thinks life is a bubble
He is the one I strive to be
He is my Luke Baranyai.

The way he takes a gentle stride
The way he mumbles but crumbles inside
He is the one I strive to be
He is my Luke Baranyai.

I want to strive for higher goals
I want to be happy and let life take its toll
Luke is the one I strive to be
Luke is my inspiration.

Peter Walker (14)
Brighouse High School, Brighouse

The Future Together

Together we want
A world without war, destruction and death
Free from hate, bitterness and malice
And an end to poverty
To lose the great sadness

Together we need
A world with equality, hope and strength
Brimming with love, life and light
And peace for everyone
To find a great happiness

Together we could
Have a world with a future, green and great
Without crime or pollution littering our planet
And see it through
To create an everlasting home

Together we will make it happen.

Eleanor Savage (13)
Brighouse High School, Brighouse

Little Girl Cry

In the dark alleyway
A small girl hides in the shadows
Hiding from a man
Which sadly is her daddy
This vandalises her heart and
Plays soccer with her confidence
Shocks and flashbacks repeat in her mind
Will she ever grown up to be happy?
Can she ever start a family?
Or will she not want to risk the pain which
Clouded over her childhood?
But every story has a happy ending, right?
There's always a light at the end of the tunnel
But this innocent little girl
Alone and just three
This sorrowful soul
That was me.

Abigail Shields (13)
Brighouse High School, Brighouse

In The Future I Know

I am the president of the United States
From poor beginnings I have risen to power
And although the United States has come far
We still have a long way to go.

In the future I hope every child has an education
Everybody has a home and clean water to drink
All children are cared for and looked after
And all sick people are nursed to health.

In the future I want there to be no more pain
No more torturing or war and
No more discrimination against anyone.

In the future I know there will be no more criminals
There will be no more disease or disasters
Everyone will reach their full potential.

This is my dream for the future.

Michael Barker (14)
Brighouse High School, Brighouse

Addiction

Madness, confusion, swirling and regret
Pressured, she is scared now, so helpless
Lashing out, screaming, stupid and upset
Controlled like a puppet, fighting to escape it.

Her attacker is demanding, pressuring her, 'take more'
He has a tight grip on her mind, how can she get out?
She breaks down, 'what did I start this for?'
But she is strong, she sees a way out.

She seeks help, and soon her attacker has fled
She feels like water bursting from a broken pipe
She warns others not to be as easily led
For she is happy now she is free.

Emily Barrett (14)
Brighouse High School, Brighouse

Dreams

Dreams are like clouds
You have lots of them but most are hard to reach
But if you believe in yourself anything is possible
The world is your oyster
Stand tall and reach your goal.

Inspiration is all you need
Give it your all and no one can complain
If you have tried your best
Then you have reached your goal.

Don't let others stop you
Don't let others put you down
Smile and your life lights up
Smile and your dreams come true.

Dreams are meant for more than just dreaming about
Make them happen!

Amelia Carter (14)
Brighouse High School, Brighouse

Where Would I Be?

I have grown up in absolute Hell
Now you have arrived, you have cured that spell
You took hold of my hands, and that was just when
Our blue and brown eyes met and you said, 'Try, try again.'

I took your advice, and look where I am now
I'm on top of the world, ready to take a bow
Not because of what I've done, but just because of you
I'm so glad I listened, my heart beats for you.

I have reached my goals and done what I can
I thank you so much, I'm your number one fan
Without you I'd be nothing, who knows where I'd be?
Right now it just feels good to accept it's you and me.

Hollie Mason (14)
Brighouse High School, Brighouse

The Child

A boy is born so small and cold
Forced out into the world
Where the cold wind blows

A young little boy, with a hungry sister
Cuddles her as the storm blows cold

He starts to work day and night
To help his family grow and fight

A sick little boy sat on his own
He has nothing to eat, he's all alone

He tries to fight it
He tries so hard
But his body gives up
He lies down and dies . . .

Help stop child poverty!

Holly Thorp (13)
Brighouse High School, Brighouse

Child Abuse

Sitting there, all alone, weeping, sobbing for its mum
Their head throbbing, room spinning
What did they do wrong? Is it their fault, who's to blame?
Shaking, they try to pick up the phone, 'This time I'll do it
I'll ring Childline.'
But by the time they dial, the monsters are back again.

Child abuse isn't nice, it's not kind and it's scary
A little child, all on its own, worrying, fretting,
'What will happen next?'
Let's help them, give them support, show them that
Someone cares.

Put a full stop.

Grace Siddle (12)
Brighouse High School, Brighouse

The Daffodil

In times of old when I was new
In careless patches through the wood
Surrounding blue primrose stood
I wore my yellow sun bonnet
I wore my greenest gown
I turned to the south wind and curtsied up and down
Those were the days, how the land has changed
Everything's rearranged
The brown soil clenches me tight
For I will carry my sword, with delight
What are these things so mighty and tall
That make me feel so insecure and small?
How can those beasts destroy something so blessed
And make it torn and distressed?
While my cowardice friends gave way
I will fight till my dying day.

Alexandra Gaukrodger (13)
Brighouse High School, Brighouse

Reflection

Glazed eyes
An absent smile
Her mind floats away
To her own sea of dreams

The golden raindrops
Slip down the flooding window
Outside the rays of sun are beaming
Onto the glistening puddles
That reflected her mood.

Her pensive eyes
Hide the wishing faith inside
As the stream of hope
Gushes down the waterfall
To reality.

Juliette Smith (13)
Brighouse High School, Brighouse

Dreaming Dreams

They say dreams never do come true
But they are wrong, I say they do.

I dream of bullying, I dream of hurt
I dream of children, they live in dirt.

I dream of my feelings, I dream of my thoughts
I dream of these things, I dream of them lots.

I dream of my loved ones, I dream of the dead
I dream of these thoughts, exploding in my head.

I dream that these things would never come true
But unfortunately, they always do.

They say dreams never do come true
But they are wrong, I say they do.

Eli Cumplido (12)
Brynteg Comprehensive School, Bridgend

A Dream Is A Dream

A dream is a dream
And your dream
Can change tomorrow.

A dream is there for a
Reason
A dream is there to be
Chased if it runs
Away
A dream is your destiny
To follow.

Everyone has a dream
And any dream is as
Big as you make it.

You may wish upon
A star
But the only way
You'll live your dream
Is to rise above it and be strong.

So in the words of Martin Luther King, 'I have a dream.'
And you may say the same words so, have faith in yourself
A dream is like a memory
It stays with you forever
Until one day, you let it go
But that would be disappointing

Wouldn't it?

Emily March (12)
Brynteg Comprehensive School, Bridgend

A Dream Like This One

Thousands of people screaming out
They shout and shout
Let me be seen
Let me be heard
Just hear my dream.

One of them could be you
Standing in the crowd
But standing proud!

Standing up for your country, religion or family
Without silence or fear
When your love is clear, anything is possible.
Yes, they could throw you in jail
'I'm guilty, I'm guilty!' you'd plead
'I'm guilty of trying to stop people's hearts bleeding!
I'm trying to help the people we need
Maybe not today
But tomorrow is another day, there's
Another way.'

Most importantly, another voice is going
To be heard, another dream
Come true.

A dream like this one.

Meghan Bryant (12)
Brynteg Comprehensive School, Bridgend

I Had A Dream

I have a dream
Where people get to live their lives peacefully
Loving and caring with no harm or corruption
Give people the chance to live their lives truly
Spend time with people you love most
Loving, caring, just the way a family should.

Jordan Tunster
Brynteg Comprehensive School, Bridgend

Poor Me . . .

Poor me, jaded me
Broken for the world to see
Evil words that swarm around
Writhing, killing
But there's no sound
Desolation's one I know
So come on kids, enjoy the show
Hit me, what have I left to lose?
Searching for these Tippexed truths,

And in despair we find ourselves
Even though we've been to Hell
We'll rise above with a light so bright
That evil cannot stand the sight
For we know love's greatest endeavour
Is to find a voice as soft as a feather
And banish hatred to its grave
With the prospect of ourselves to save
We convert this hope to self control
To stopper up our own black hole
And even though it will be hard
With this I know we'll travel far
Even though joy's ripped at the seams
This, my dear, is my only dream.

Megan Bierney (13)
Brynteg Comprehensive School, Bridgend

I Have A Dream

I had a dream that people would love
Me for who I am, and not for who I'm not.
I had a dream that I was a star and I went far.
I had a dream that the world was peaceful and kind.
But i guess I'll have to wait for another dream . . .

Cory Parry (12)
Brynteg Comprehensive School, Bridgend

Anything's Possible

I have a dream where there are no more guns or war
A world without cancer or diseases any more
Where people are happy and friendly all day
A place that old and homeless people can stay.

I have a dream where there's no more racism or crime
Something good's gonna happen in a matter of time
Whatever your dream is, don't be ashamed
Always be proud of what you've gained.

I have a dream where everyone's the same
Not to be the guy at the back of the train
To be the guy standing out from the crowd
Who's not afraid to speak out loud.

I hope this message has opened up your eyes
To not be afraid, not scream, not cry
If you have a dream, go ahead and chase it
As long as you remember the sky's the limit.

The meaning of this poem was to inspire you
So when you're older you can inspire people too
As I come to the end you can make anew
All I can say now is dreams do come true.

Marcus Cheung
Brynteg Comprehensive School, Bridgend

I Dream

I dream that everyone will believe in themselves
I dream that we will all be equal
Just because of the colour of our skin
It doesn't mean that we aren't all God's children
I dream that no one will make fun of each other
Just because they are slow, dumb or handicapped
I have a dream that one day everyone will love each other
No matter what they look like.

Kierra Williams
Brynteg Comprehensive School, Bridgend

A Dream In A Box

The girl stood on the box
The box was small
Like her.
She opened her lips
But no sound came out
The protest around was
A horrible sight
She closed her eyes and wished
For a world of light
And happiness
She left behind the unpleasant
Protest of the night
She joined a world of hopes and
Dreams.
She sent her world to jail
For its hurtful actions and words
The world was soon sorted out
No war. No fights.
The girl stood on her box and knew
Actions
Spoke louder
Than words.

Nicola Casling (11)
Brynteg Comprehensive School, Bridgend

Imagine . . .

Imagine a world where there was no war
Imagine a world where no one was poor
Imagine lives are not lost in wars we caused
And where all our problems are solved
Where family and friends do not fight to solve their problems
One word can save a life
Say what you feel, make it heard, make it real
Imagine a world where your words are listened to.

Joshua Thomas
Brynteg Comprehensive School, Bridgend

Wishing For A Dream

I have a dream that the world
Will be a better place to live in
No pollution, no war and no bombs
Please help me find the solution.

I wish we could stand up to our enemies
To make peace not war
Not judging people by the colour of their skin
Please help me find a solution.

In my dream I will live in a
World with no knives or violence
Gangs will be groups of happy people
Please help me find a solution.

The streets will be clean
Shops will be full
And there will be jobs for everyone
I really wish my dream would come true.

Charlotte Beech (12)
Brynteg Comprehensive School, Bridgend

I Have A Dream

When something goes wrong, don't put your head down
Stick up for your rights, don't get into fights.

Men and women, black and white
All stand together, you know its right.

Gone are the days when we should be kept apart
Time to make a fresh new start.

Inside us all is a special dream
Don't keep quiet, let it out
Scream!
Use your voice to state your case
We are all equal in the human race.

Steven Gauci (12)
Brynteg Comprehensive School, Bridgend

I Have A Dream

An amazing dream or a worst nightmare?
The touch of angels' light feathers in all their glory

A spark of lightning when touched
A shivery feeling going down your spine like
Someone is there watching you.

An angel from above coming down to bring
Me to Heaven.

But strangely looked like a devil coming
To torture me forever.

Or God taking me to Heaven to live in
Happiness.

Who took me somewhere? Where did I go?
Was it God or the devil?

Was it a dream or a worst nightmare?

Sara Kirk (13)
Brynteg Comprehensive School, Bridgend

Give This World Some Peace

I'm going to dream a dream
Until my dream comes true
Give the poor some food
Let them live their lives like us.

Think of all our men in Iraq
Whilst we live our lives
Some are losing their lives
Whilst fighting for us.

You could live today
But die tomorrow
So dream *your* dream
And believe it can come true.

Emma Johnson (12)
Brynteg Comprehensive School, Bridgend

Equal

Every night the same
The same dream, same hope, same faith
Trusting the world to one day redeem itself
To make my dream, reality.

I'm a small girl in a big world
My voice, overpowered among most, will
Someday be heard
And my wish granted at last.

My wish:
No more tears or fears
No more people cry and no more people die
Because someone, somewhere was too
Afraid to make a difference.
Finally, everyone equal.

That is my dream.

Holly Tyler (12)
Brynteg Comprehensive School, Bridgend

A Big Dream

I had a dream
That there was no pollution, no poverty, no war
I had a dream
That we all lived together happily
That guns and bombs were no more
I had a dream
That I could change the world around
And people would help me
I had a dream
That someone would listen to me
And it wouldn't matter
That I am so small.

Lola Bridgeman (12)
Brynteg Comprehensive School, Bridgend

Dream On!

I have a dream
A very strong dream
One where everything mean
Goes away
Far away
Where we can say goodbye to
All the guns and pollution
But I know that's all an
Illusion
Even so, hold on tight to your
Dream till the day you die
Because it might just come
True
So dream on
Dream on forever!

Amber Dare-Edwards (11)
Brynteg Comprehensive School, Bridgend

My Dream

A dream for the world to be happy
Boys, girls, ladies and gentlemen
A dream for no pollution or poverty
But for the world to be saved
No sadness or death, no upsets or crying
But most of all, no more dying.

People smiling, playing football in the park
Playing and playing until it goes dark
People having fun while living wealthily
Talking to mates
On romantic dates.

Life's like a holiday, so enjoy in the right way
So this is goodbye, but have a nice day.

Rory Nicholls
Brynteg Comprehensive School, Bridgend

Have Faith

Have faith in the world
Have faith in its people
To put things right
Where good is forever
And evil is thwarted by those who are pure hearted.

Have faith in people to stop slavery and end wars
Where no one is more important than the other.

Have faith in the world to stop the different races fighting
Believe in a world where no matter who or what we are
We are friends.

But to make this happen you need to

Have faith!

Callum Jones (12)
Brynteg Comprehensive School, Bridgend

Fantasy Dream

I went to bed one gloomy night
I saw the glowing moon
I shut my eyes and dreamed of gold
I dreamed about huge dragons and white unicorns so fine
The dragons flew above the pink sparkling sky
And above the cotton candy clouds
A dragon was bleeding and hurt
It was Man who killed the last dragon
The unicorn died of a broken heart and sorrow
But they were reunited in Heaven

They died but lived a fantasy dream.

Bronwyn Howie
Brynteg Comprehensive School, Bridgend

Dream Time

Dreams are like birds
That soar and land into reality
Dreams take you by your hand
And walk you through your deepest fears
Dreams happen in words and actions
But take just seconds to change a life, a scene, a world
A dream is confidence, a dream is hope
And without dreams no one will cope
Without dreams the world wouldn't be where it is today
No imagination and not a hope to be found
Do you have a dream?

Alys Harrop
Brynteg Comprehensive School, Bridgend

I Have A Dream

I hope that I'll be free one day
But at the moment I'm not getting paid
As I'm in jail for not saying why.

So I watch people freely live while I watch
The misery is there
I'll find the way out someday
Somehow.

So till that day I will wait
And wait
And wait for the sun to shine.

Courtney Rich
Brynteg Comprehensive School, Bridgend

Imagine

One world, one word, one dream . . .

One world
So many voices
Believe and you could change everything.

Imagine changing wrong to right
Imagine being the light of the world
Imagine speaking aloud to millions
Imagine believing, trying and succeeding
Imagine the world changing because of you
Imagine . . .

Eve Thomas
Brynteg Comprehensive School, Bridgend

Don't Forget Your Dreams!

Don't forget your dreams
Whatever they are
No matter how big or small you are
Everybody counts
The world should be equal
With all the differences in it
Don't give up
Keep on trying
Chase your dream to the end
Remember you only get *one* chance.

Tyler Harrison (12)
Brynteg Comprehensive School, Bridgend

I Have A Dream

I have a dream to make an ice cream
The biggest you've ever seen.

It would reach up high, almost to the sky
And taste of strawberry, raspberry and
Chocolate, or even all three.

You decide which tastes the best and
It will fill your mouth, great
Intense.

Cerysanne Jeffrey
Brynteg Comprehensive School, Bridgend

I Had A Dream

I had a dream last night
I dreamt the world was a better place
There was no war and there was peace on Earth
There was no poverty and everyone was treated the same
The air was clean and there was no pollution
And the environment was healthy
I dreamt the world was a better place.

Chloe Rosser (11)
Brynteg Comprehensive School, Bridgend

I Dreamt A Dream

I had a dream I could live a dream
I had a dream I was in my dream scene
I dreamt I could run fast
I dreamt I could have a fun blast
I dreamt that none of my friends would end up being in a cast
I had a dream I would never be last.
I dreamt a dream.

Jay Coombes (12)
Brynteg Comprehensive School, Bridgend

A Big Dream

I dreamt that there was no pollution
And there was a cure for every illness around the world
I dream that rainforests stop getting cut down
And everyone looks after each other.

Rhys Hulme
Brynteg Comprehensive School, Bridgend

The Dream I Have

The dream I have is a world free of corruption
The people around me hold hands, not guns
The dream I have is not easy to come true
I hope it comes true in the future.

Michael Short
Brynteg Comprehensive School, Bridgend

Capture The Dream!

The time has come, it's finally here
You are at the starting line
Get ready, get set, go!
Capture the dream!

Luke Rees-Davies (12)
Brynteg Comprehensive School, Bridgend

Dream Wishing

I have a dream . . .
If I had three wishes,
I would wish for a million more,
Cos I have a lot to look forward to,
To change in the world.

Cure cancer,
Prevent and bar AIDS,
Stop swine flu,
Help the less privileged,
Halt all diseases,
Best of all prolong lives.

For real charity begins at home,
Giving will not hurt,
Helping the homeless,
Donate and find family for them,
For I know they are one of us,
This you will find if you open my heart.

Nobody needs pity,
All we need is your love,
Cos love can change the world,
Step by step we can overcome evil,
Making the best of today,
I am sure love can rule the world.

Now that I have one more wish left,
I would ask for a million more,
But that will be ungrateful,
My last wish is to give love to everyone,
Peace and joy with understanding,
And that is my dream . . .

Rhoda Oluwadunbarin (13)
Cedar Mount High School, Manchester

I Have A Dream

I have a dream
To be the best
To save the world
And all the rest.

Building planes
Flying cars
Sofas that sing
Medical discoveries
All this I plan to do
Because . . .
I have a dream.

I have a dream
To see the world
From continent to continent
To see people and go places
Trying new things
Cos that's all there is.

French boys
And summers in the sun
Canapés and cocktails
Shopping and partying
Laughing and smiling
All these I dream to do.

I have a dream
To be the best
To be myself
To be great in life
I have a dream.

Temiloluwa Daike (14)
Cedar Mount High School, Manchester

Dreams Can Come True

I have a dream that I could be a nurse
Looking after children, working
Working hard to care for them
Sweating for love and care
And that's why I dream to
Be a nurse.

I have another dream
A dream that I could be a doctor
Examine the patient and go to
Another mystery to solve
The people who inspire me
Are all of the doctors
'Cause if it wasn't for them
We wouldn't have any medicine
Or machines to help us.

My last dream
The last dream is that I could be
A successful business woman
All these things inspire me
Because I know that one
Person is always gonna be
There and it is my . . .
Mum!

Amal Nouh (14)
Cedar Mount High School, Manchester

I Have A Dream

I have a dream that war will end
I have a dream that peace will commend
I have a dream that guns disappear
I have a dream that love will appear

What I wish to happen is that knives will blur,
What I wish to happen is that peace will occur,
What I wish to happen is that my dreams come true,
What I wish to happen is that my dreams come through.

When I see it on the telly
I just rub my belly
War goes on till they die
Just like a frog and a fly

I have a dream
I want it to gleam
I have a dream
Please make it gleam

I have a dream that war will end
I have a dream that peace will commend
I have a dream that guns disappear
I have a dream, love please appear.

James Collantine (12)
Cedar Mount High School, Manchester

Prejudice, Poetry And Dreams

I want to end poverty now
But we all have to know how
Got to share the money
'Cause poverty ain't funny
To overcome prejudice
You've got to stand up for each other
Like brother and sister.
I have a dream that all dignity will be redeemed.

Rafiq Oladujoye (13)
Cedar Mount High School, Manchester

My Perfect Mum!
(Dedicated to Michelle Humphries)

My mum loves me, I love her too
I know that this love is true
If you saw us you would see
That she means the world to me.

She's as pretty as a rose
And she knows
She watches me grow
And the whole world should know.

She tells me to fulfil my dreams
She's as bright as a sunbeam
I dance all day, I dance all night
And she's there making it right.

This is for you Mum
And I want you to have fun
For all the love and care you give
I'm so thankful that you live.

I love you,
You know it's true
I just want to say thank you!

Paige Humphries (13)
Cedar Mount High School, Manchester

A Dream

I have a dream that gun crime will end
That love and peace will commend
I have a dream that people will live
And can stay with
Family and friends
And can make amends.

I have a dream guns will end.

Keeley Fogg (12)
Cedar Mount High School, Manchester

Dreams

I have a dream
I want to become a doctor
I got inspired by my father
Who takes being healthy as one of
The important things in life.

Sometimes going to the GP,
Like a snail that has no house.
Crying, shouting, screaming,
Injection being given to the patient.

The sudden rush of fortune,
Giving children stress.
Voices echo like an angry cloud,
Old, young, teenagers going to the doctor.

I have a dream
I will have my own and the best house, cars and money in life.
I have a dream.
I will come out in flying colours
I have a dream.
I pray all my dreams shall come to life
These are my dreams.

Mariam Oyebanji (13)
Cedar Mount High School, Manchester

Untitled

I have a dream we can stop bullying
I have a dream to stop people from suffering
I have a dream to stop people from being afraid.
Stop people from tormenting
I have a dream,
I have a dream,
To stop bullying.

Louise Baker (12)
Cedar Mount High School, Manchester

My Dream

I want to be an artist
And draw all my life
Earn lots and lots and money
And have a beautiful wife

I'm going to buy a car
It will be very, very fast
If I'm ever in a race
I will never finish last

I'm going to buy a house
And fill up all my land
Hello my name is Marcus
Please shake my hand

I'm going to have good style
And wear different types of suits
I will always attend my meetings
And will always salute.

Marcus Cunningham (14)
Cedar Mount High School, Manchester

My Dreams

To be an artist that is my dream,
To use colours like orange, yellow and green,
I aim to be just as good as my dad,
'Cause right now compared to him I just look bad.
I aim to have money and a peaceful life,
With a statue in my garden I sculpted with a sculptor's knife.
I dream to be a tattooist not just an artist,
I dream to have money and a bike to get to the parties,
I like poems but that's just a hobby,
It sounds posh but I ain't snobby,
That's my future and I need GCSEs
You'll see I'll get two As, one star and about three Cs.

Cammeron Moore (13)
Cedar Mount High School, Manchester

Pet's Pain

Lonely animal in an alley
But to small little Rover it's a lonely valley
Abandoned at Christmas like so many others
With rising figures of this it's like nobody bothers.

Tied to a post, imprisoned by fate
Sitting alone in a terrible state
A whimper in a hole, alone in the dark
Silence and quiet except a lonely bark

Animals abandoned, there are so many
And the figures just seem to rise quite steadily
So look after your pet, show it some love
And try to act as the divine forces above

Keep animals indoors and well looked after
Humanity could you be any dafter
To not see our beloved pets' pain
And to let this poem be written in rain?

Zachary Curran (13)
Cedar Mount High School, Manchester

Untitled

This person inspires me the most
That's why I have a lot of post

This person has a lot of surprises
But never ends up in demise

He may not be popular
But he shows true colour

He has three kids and is my mum's best friend
Bu he will never let his guard down till the end

He's my true friend and is not to be known.

Shaun Gleitze (13)
Cedar Mount High School, Manchester

Unite For Peace

I have a dream that war will end
I have a dream that guns disappear
I have a dream that we're all friends
I have a dream that peace will commend.

I have a dream that we unite as one
I have a dream that racism's gone
I have a dream that everyone's respected
I have a dream that no one's neglected.

I have a dream that everyone loves
No more suffering, no more guns
I have a dream that no one's afraid
No matter where they live or what's their age.

I have a dream that war will end
I have a dream that guns will disappear
I have a dream that we're all friends
I have a dream that people will commend.

Samuel Marrett (12)
Cedar Mount High School, Manchester

My Dream

I have a dream to have a job in football
Whether it is a manager, coach or player
On the dole never; I want a good job
And to be happy forever.

Ronaldo, Crouch, Beckham and my mum
Inspire me to act on this dream.
I can imagine the beam of the floodlights
As I walk out of the tunnel for the first time.
Here I am living my dream
Now I hear the crowd roaring and chanting my name.

Aidan Rainford (14)
Cedar Mount High School, Manchester

I Have A Dream

I have a dream we will all live as one
To see the world's beauty, mysteries and fun
To end all the things like famine and war
To live our life to its fullest and more

All around the world there are endless sights
Of people always getting into fights
Domestic violence wherever you go
All these things are wrong and you need to know

There's enough food in this world to feed us
So why do most of us make such a fuss?
When in other countries they don't get much
To feed themselves, their families and such

So live your life without any regrets
Don't be a big bully handing out threats
Lend a hand to the ones that are in need
You never know what might happen indeed.

Minh Tram Phan (13)
Cedar Mount High School, Manchester

A Dream

I have a dream that I have a big house,
Fast car and a very good job in art,
Kids, lots of money and a very, very happy life.
Friends who inspire me, a teacher who inspires me by helping me,
Family, another artist who inspires me.
George O'Keefe, he inspires me.

Marcin Szwanka (14)
Cedar Mount High School, Manchester

I Have A Dream

I have a dream
To be a successful nurse.
I have a dream
To treat sickness in pills.
I have a dream
To make people happy and feel better.
I have a dream
To go to college and university.
I have a dream
To make enough money to take care of my children.
I have a dream
To have a big house like a celebrity.
I have a dream
To make my mum happy.
I have a dream
To be like my mum 'cause she is a nurse.
I have a dream.

Aishat Siyanbola (14)
Cedar Mount High School, Manchester

My Dream

I have a dream
A dream to be a nurse
To help look after people who are ill
Who will need my help.

The person who inspire me to achieve my dream is my auntie Rita
The reason she inspires me is because she has dedicated years of her life to help people, to make them better.
She is like Florence Nightingale who helped lots of people get better
She is like an angel from Heaven who has come down to Earth to nurse patients back to health.

I hope that one day I can be a better nurse than my auntie Rita
So I can achieve the things that my auntie never has
So I can look after patients and dedicate years of my life to help them get better.
So I can make my auntie proud.

Vanessa Sharp (13)
Cedar Mount High School, Manchester

Mr Right

I have a dream to find Mr Right.
Hope everything will go as I plan.
He's my shining light.
He will always be my number one fan.
I will always be there for him, forever and ever.
I wanna be the one he calls his wife.
The amount of time we will argue will be never.
He will always be in my life.
No one will break us up now.
I want to be the one to call him my boo,
Wow!
I can't believe how much this means to me.
When I see him am gonna feel free!

Tinotenda Muchirawehondo (12)
Cedar Mount High School, Manchester

The Dream Of Peace

I have a dream that one day the world will gleam.
No wars but peace, love will increase.
But how can you stop a war when there's cruel intentions with
                                          many imperfections?
Though that's only procedure with a strategic seizure.

Iraq or Afghanistan, you'll always have to stick to the plan.
That's the discipline of being a man.
Bullets flying around me everywhere.
I have a family but what does the enemy care?
Soon it will be in the news tomorrow,
God there will be so much sorrow.
As the brave patriot who dies in battle,
When will the world change? When will I see it rattle?
I have a dream that one day the world will gleam.
We shall all work together as a team.

Jubaer Alam (13)
Cedar Mount High School, Manchester

The Bully

I come out hearing the laughter
And seeing the golden ray of the sun
But now all I see is him with a plaster
On his face, holding a young boy clutching a bun
'He' was forcing the boy to give it to him
But no answer came
So 'he' decided to pin
Him to the wall and call him lame
Grabbing everything he owned
And threw him to the ground
Leaving to get an ice cream cone
Deserting him with nothing but a pound
Now I want to stop bullying
That is what I am planning.

Thu Ngoc Nguyen (13)
Cedar Mount High School, Manchester

Helping

My life is difficult to believe
Sometimes I can't keep it up my sleeve
But only one thing is helping me out
And now I don't need to doubt.

Only one person can change my mind
And another person can be too kind
To make me change and not be greedy
And different and selfish and not be needy.

Now being different isn't so bad
I am now happy and not sad
Thanks you my family and friends, I was ready
To choose three people to be my bezzies.

Thu, Minh Tram and Arthur are the people who tend
To be my best friends till the end.

Al Shady Conteh
Cedar Mount High School, Manchester

Life War

I can't wait to see my child
This place is so wild
Bombs and guns
But the only thing I want to see is my son
But will I make it out
Or will I have to shout
For my life
Just to see my wife
Do you think I will get sent home
Or just end up dead and all alone?
Maybe I might wake up and see the sun
Tomorrow maybe I won't
But I want to make it
Without needing an emergency kit.

Rudeen Maamoo (13)
Cedar Mount High School, Manchester

The Boxer's Story

'Matthew, Matthew!'
The crowd chants my name as I step up to the ring.
My opponent looks at me from across the ring and smirks.
I smile to myself, I can win, I can win.
I get myself focused on the target and I visualise the win.
The referee calls us up to the centre, '4, 3, 2, 1, fight!'
We circle each other like lions.
It was all over in a flash.
My opponent was on the floor out cold
The crowd cheering.
My dad shouted, 'Well done Son, I knew you could do it!
You're a real winner, a champion!'
Me and my dad had been training for this day for three years
My dad pushing me to the limits
'Work hard and you will achieve great things!' and he was right!

Matthew Cook (14)
Cedar Mount High School, Manchester

My Mum . . .
(Written for Caroline Jane Martin)

I wrote this song to show my care
For my mum, my cuddly bear.
She's as pretty as a golden flower
And definitely has a lot of power.
I love my mum loads and loads,
She's not like an old, ugly toad.
I love hearing her laughter,
It makes me smile for a long time after.
She helps me out
When I'm in doubt
And sticks up for me when things are wrong
And that is why I wrote this song.

Afra Martin (12)
Cedar Mount High School, Manchester

I Have A Dream

When I see you on the telly
I want to be just like you
I have a dream that I could be famous too
With all the paparazzi in my face
Living life at my own pace
As pretty as a flower and as busy as a bee
I never thought a famous person could be like me
All women are beautiful just like you
I want to be beautiful, what can I do?
Being friendly gets you far
Like having money and big trendy cars
You inspire me to be as busy as a bee
So I will look as pretty as can be.

Darian Ankers (12)
Cedar Mount High School, Manchester

The Travelling Man

Not thinking what could have been
Go now, see what's to be seen
The sights, the sounds, smells and tastes,
Do them now with much haste.

The planet's an amazing place
If only everyone could pack their suitcase
Cairo in Egypt, Tokyo in Japan
Visit these places every child, woman and man.

But instead people stay where they are
Not daring to travel afar
They sit at home as time elapses
They go here, perhaps.

Matthew Sean Wright (12)
Filey Secondary School, Filey

In The Heat Of Battle!

Click, click, the magazine slips in
The safety catch off
Peering down the sight of a barren landscape
Suddenly a shout
A head emerges encased with tin
Wracked with fear
'What will we do? They're coming over!'

Green-clad warriors emerge in line
Rifles in hands, bayonets fixed
Standing there, feeling sick
Mouth dry and trembling
'Will this by my glory bed?
Or will I turn and flee?'

The enemy marches on
The machine guns chatter, the cannons roar
Crack! Thump! Bullets pass overhead
I look down the sight asking myself
'Do I really want to fight?'

They keep on coming, they are close now
Hands are shaking, stomach churning
Will I die today? Frozen with fear.

Clutching my chest, it's oozing blood
Hard to breathe, panic stricken
'Stretcher bearer, stretcher bearer!'
'Don't let my friend die!'
Eyesight fading, cold inside
Lifted with care, a friendly face
Mons angels above me, feeling safe
Now I can rest in this better place.

Alex Low (13)
Filey Secondary School, Filey

Apocalypse

The sky was crimson
But the sun had gone.
Not a thing
Breathes on this land.

It came and went
Destroying all.
Making life Hell
For us all.

The trees are red
But not with water:
The ground is sodden
With our blood.

We fought its might
But with no hope
For it was
A hopeless fight.

It swept through
Our cities and towns
Crushing all
In it's path.

It laid great
Armies asunder
For none could survive
Its mighty wrath.

It was, after all
Mankind's worst day
For it was
The Apocalypse.

Alan Jones (12)
Filey Secondary School, Filey

I Once Had A Dream

I once had a dream
That I was running a race:
Sun in my eyes,
Wind in my face.

I once had a dream
That I was running on a track:
Stamina disappearing -
But there was no turning back.

I once had a dream
That I was winning by a mile,
But the finish line,
Was not for a while.

I once had a dream
That I slipped in the mud;
I tried to stop myself
But I landed with a thud.

I once had a dream
That lots of people passed.
I tried to catch them up -
But no doubt, I was last.

I once had a dream
That I picked up the pace:
Getting faster and faster
Until I was first place.

I once had a dream
That I crossed the finish line.
I had won the race!
The trophy was mine!

Heather Pearson (11)
Filey Secondary School, Filey

Missing

Lying there,
Cold and alone:
Is there anyone out there?
Is that a noise?
A whisper; a cry,
Is there anyone out there?
Trees move in the wind,
Scary faces haunt my mind;
Lying there cold and alone.
Is there anyone out there?
The cracking of footsteps;
The murmur of voices.
Have they found me?
Is there anyone out there?
The wind swells the voices.
Cold, sharp pains
Pulsate through me.
Have they found me?
Can I call for help?
What if they miss me?
Walk past, carry on?
I croak out the impossible word,
'Help!'
All falls silent; am I safe
Or is my mind crazy?
Is there really
Anyone out there?

Lucy Miller (15)
Filey Secondary School, Filey

Nightmare At War

The fierce roaring of the open fire
The loud screaming from near and far
The whistle of the wind
The trees falling in the night
Made you think:
Will there ever be peace?

The crashing of the planes
Out in the town
The murmuring children
Whimpering in their beds
Banging and banging
Made you think:
Will there ever be peace?

Parents cooking over open fires
Tears oozing from their eyes
The smell of smoke
Children coughing and spluttering
Made you think:
Will there ever be peace?

Thudding bombs
Vivid lights
Outside my dark room
Shivering with fright
Made me think:
Will there ever be peace?

Charlotte Donkin (12)
Filey Secondary School, Filey

Lost, Lost

Lost, lost, wherever I am
There's no one here but me
I am all alone in the dark
Whatever will I do?

What's that over there
On the horizon
That speck on that hill?
I will have to go and see

Finally I am over there
Whatever will it be?
But no, no it's only a cat
Now all my hopes are lost

I wonder now what will I do
Because all my hopes are lost
All the chances ruined
I might as well just give up

Yes, yes, finally a helicopter
I wonder if he can see me
Finally he's stopped, he's landed
My luck has turned to gold

Lost, lost, now I'm not.

John Oakley (13)
Filey Secondary School, Filey

Comparison

The youngest of three
It was never going to be easy
Both sisters at university
And then there's me

What will you do when you're older?
Going to be like your big sister?
I sidle away. The big sisters are here
What else am I going to do?

I don't have a clue
I'm only fourteen
I want to leave school
And 'enjoy my youth'

I'm not a linguist
Or a scientist
I'm not a farmer
Or a land surveyor

At the end of the day
I am myself
And I don't know how to say
I am who I am, don't put me in comparison.

Annabel Coleman (14)
Filey Secondary School, Filey

A World Of Reality

I had a dream
That all men lived together in peace.
A world without poverty or starvation.
A world without wars, fighting and guns.
A world of peace.

I had a nightmare
That all men had enemies.
A world with poverty and starvation.
A world with wars or fighting.
A world of fear.

A world of reality.

Tom Crookes (11)
Filey Secondary School, Filey

Freedom

Freedom is the best
Stronger than slavery
Better than cruelty
Warmer than wealth
Greater than possessions
Dear as love
Safer than imprisonment
Closer than friends
Worth more than anything
Because without freedom
We are nothing.

Charlotte Metcalfe (12)
Filey Secondary School, Filey

I Have A Dream

People will stop polluting the world
Only electric cars allowed
Prisoners will get a second chance once they become civilised
The prime minister should be fired
Replaced by someone better
No more taxes
Houses, food and drink for the homeless
The animals will all have homes to go to
No more poachers in the world.

World peace and every person
Even different skin colours play as friends
There will be no more violence and more security for people
There will be no more gangs, no more weapons or war

Earth will be a peaceful world
People will play outside more
People will stop destroying our ecosystem.

Cameron Carpenter (12)
Fosse Way School, Radstock

I Have A Dream

I want the world to be a safer place.
I want the poor people to eat well, wear better clothes and earn some money.
I want the curse of floods and the hazards to come to an end.
I want all the flowers to bloom for the poor people
I want all the pets to have safer homes.
I want more charity for the poor people and the pets who lost their homes.
I want to hand over the medicines for the poor people to erase viruses, flu, cancer and heart disease.
I want to say to all the people of every country that no matter how you look, you're still the same person.

Zoë Wilding (12)
Fosse Way School, Radstock

I Have A Dream

I have a dream where people could stop wars and have peace.
I wish we could stop killing others for no reason.
I wish we could stop killing animals.
I wish people could stop beating others up.
I wish I could stop pollution.
I wish we could all work together and help each other and have peace.

Georgina Hart (12)
Fosse Way School, Radstock

I Had A Dream

I wish there will be no more wars
All jobs will pay the same
People in charge will not make war
Everyone will get treated the same
Everyone will be much friendlier to each other.

Matthew Collins (14)
Fosse Way School, Radstock

Akon

Through your life in jail
All the pain you went through
Only because you were treated differently
Hoping to become a better person

Visitation no longer came by
Everyone forgot about you
Every cell was getting empty
You were left all alone

You didn't give up even through hard times
All the excitement, wishing every day would be better
Found your music talent
You were now valuable to everybody

Tried to help other people with your song lyrics
For them to get a better life
Thanks to you Akon
People's lives are now better.

Percy Shey
Hodge Hill Sports & Enterprise College, Birmingham

Sound Sleep

So far away from war,
I sleep soundly every night
I rise each morning,
Grateful to the smiling light.

Often, I think of them -
The children in the papers,
To me, merely lines,
And nameless pictures.

Children in darkness,
Surrounded by fear,
They know they can scream
But no one will hear.

Without protection,
Weakened and frayed,
With no one to trust,
Left in disarray . . .

I wonder, sometimes,
If they can sleep as well,
If they wake up to alarm clocks,
Or to something else . . .

Do they think that the monsters slipped
Out from their dreams
To come and haunt
Their reality?

Can they ever sleep?

And I wonder if someone will save them,
Send the monsters back to forgotten dreams,
I wonder if someone will save them,
And finally leave room for Peace.

I hope that one day the children
Will wake up to the Innocence of Peace,
To morning light, to happiness,
After a night of sound sleep.

Navya Myneni (17)
International School of Hyderabad, Hyderabad, India

I Have A Dream

Before the morning mist settles
On the dew-encrusted leaves,
She lies in her bed,
Fast asleep,
Enveloped in a dream.

Perhaps her mind ought not to wander
But the only place
Where she is truly free
Is in her slumber,
Where she is not judged
By shrewd glances
And malicious men.

The chains that bind her
Snap in two,
And her bastard child
Is born anew,
Gifted with the untainted touch
Of a mother
Who is not a whore.

But even as she sleeps,
Untroubled in her visions of freedom.
She cannot help but marvel -
The men who claim to be whole,
Righteous and religious,
Always succumb to her unnerving beauty
As the stars kill the day.

How can she be classed
As the lowest of the low,
When she only does what she does
In order to make a living?
Harlotry is just another job
And she had the skills to do it.

She'll pop another few pills
If it means that she can never wake up.

Valmik Kumar (16)
International School of Hyderabad, Hyderabad, India

*Young*Writers

I Dream

I dream
We are the future

I dream
We are the world

I dream
No more racism

I dream
The pollution gone . . . and global warming gone . . .

I dream
No eruptions, no volcanoes, no Earth movement, no earthquakes

I dream
A world without wars, without danger, without drugs

I dream
I was asleep and something happened

I dream
We will all join hands to make a better world

I dream of
Peace in the whole world

I know we are the future.

Clementina Orte Loustau (11)
Ivy Thomas Memorial School, Montevideo, Uruguay

I Have A Dream

I hope to see
This world without wars

I do expect
This world without violence

I do expect
People no longer offended by
The colour of their skin

I hope to see
People no longer dying of thirst or hunger

I do expect
A peaceful world

I hope to see
Animals no longer being killed

These are my dreams
to make a better world.

Mariana Viglietti Viera (11)
Ivy Thomas Memorial School, Montevideo, Uruguay

I Have A Dream

I believe
In a better future

I believe
Pollution will one day stop

I believe
Violence will one day stop

I believe
Global warming will one day stop

I believe
People will not die of thirst or hunger

I believe
There will be no discrimination

I believe
In a better future.

Paula Dibueno Camano (11)
Ivy Thomas Memorial School, Montevideo, Uruguay

How I Wish . . .

How I wish
There wasn't any fighting or wars,
That slavery disappeared.

How I wish
There wasn't any pollution, hunger or racism,
That poverty didn't exist.

How I wish
There wasn't any abuse of children and adults,
That everyone could be free.

How I wish
This world of injustice and suffering changed
With a blink of my eyes, in peace.

Irina Peyrot (11)
Ivy Thomas Memorial School, Montevideo, Uruguay

I Have A Dream

I have a dream to be rich and famous;
I have a dream to have an A-list status.
I have a dream in my head,
It starts when I go to bed.
I have a dream that people will link arms
And stand together, forever.
I have a dream to have lots of money,
I have a dream it will always be sunny.
I have a dream to be with you forever,
I don't care what they say, I'll never waiver.
I have a dream that people will live in peace,
No more war or crime, no more tears in children's eyes.
I have a dream never to cry, never to be hurt or even die.
I have a dream one day people will see;
See what you really mean to me.

Amy Grana De La Pena (12) & Leomi Windsor (13)
James Brindley School, Birmingham

I Have A Dream

I have a dream
The world will turn into vanilla ice cream.

When I look at the sky
I will see steak and kidney Pukka pies.

When I go to Game
People will treat me with fame.

When I become an actor
My act will be the dictator.

When I go to school
Kids will say 'Garry's cool!'

I have a dream.

Garry Jack (13)
James Brindley School, Birmingham

Dreaming

D is for determination
R is for being ready
E is for enjoyment in life
A is for achievement
M is for the happy moments you've had
I is for investing for the future
N is for never give up
G is for getting up and looking forward to the day

I have a dream.

Luke Price (14)
James Brindley School, Birmingham

I Have A Dream

I have a dream
That there will be no poor
People but more rich people
I have a dream
That I will be a pro footballer
Like you, we all have a dream.

Ashley Bridges (13)
James Brindley School, Birmingham

Nature Leaving

Playing outside
No trees, no plants
I want to have some nature here

More and more buildings
Less and less nature
Why, why, why?

Nature, nature please don't go away
Nature, nature stay by me
Nature, nature please don't hide

Cars, cars, cars
Cars are everywhere
Polluting the beautiful nature and Earth

Nature, nature, I am coming
Nature, nature I will help you
I will help you as much as I can

People, people come and help
People, come help the Earth and nature
Nature stay strong

Trees, flowers, nature
Why are you leaving so fast?
We will save you fast

Planting new trees
Planting new dreams
Planting nature just for you

And soon there will be new trees
New trees and new flowers
Nature you got saved

Saved from us
We are happy you are still here
We hope you are happy too.

Nina-Louise Dean (12)
Munich International School, Starnberg, Germany

Help Me

Hearing the shouts, the footsteps and crashes
I run upstairs, leaving the bashes
'You can run but you can't Hide!'
He reminds me but still I try
As I run, on my back I feel the slashes.

My mum has gone, just left one day
Knowing my sistEr and I will pay
He threatens, beats and sneers
I see the bloodshot eyes through my tears
I know that all I can do is pray.

Helpless and lost is aLl I know
Hearing the abuse, saying I'm slow
I try to escape but he's too good
I just wish I understood
I just wish I could say no

After being beaten for years and years
I got helP and let go of all my fears
I revealed all his crimes
Those horrible times
Threats and abuse screamed in my ears

Now that awful man is past
Finally gone for good, at last
Though I'm still afraid
I will be betrayed
He will coMe back
I will have to think fast

But now I can live my life
Without him or his wife
In pEace and quiet
Without a riot
At last my heart doesn't have his knife.

Francesca Buckley (13)
Munich International School, Starnberg, Germany

My Mother

Mother!
I hear the sounds like metal
Coming from outside the forest
In my mother's eyes I can see fear
The smooth wind streams the palm trees mildly.

Mother!
Disquiet is flowing through my blood
People? My father? A stranger?
All that is shooting from my head
Not knowing what is going on.

Mother!
My mother points at a tree!
It is a sign. For what? Danger?
Climbing up the tree
I realise I am on a beautiful, big palm tree.

Mother!
People. Strangers. Something wrong in the forest
My heart starts to beat faster
I hear a loud shot and see my lovely mother
Dead? Alive? What has happened?

Mother!
Everything so quiet now
I love her so much and now she is gone
Only because we were near their palm trees
Strangers, why can't you leave us alone?

David Winokurow (15)
Munich International School, Starnberg, Germany

Poverty

Full of it in the world
They are not lucky
Like us
They cannot afford to buy three meals a day
Unlike us
They don't have a roof over them
Unlike us
I have a dream
That people who are not able to afford food
Like us
Are able to afford to buy food
Like us
Live in a home
Like us
And have a blanket to keep them warm
Like us
Have a house even if it is very small
And have a bed to lie on
Like us
If this were to happen
There wouldn't be that much fighting
Which would make the world a better place.

Chase Edwards (12)
Munich International School, Starnberg, Germany

I Mourn

I do not dream
Since the day
My mother died
And swept away

I only imagine
How it feels
To have a dream
That lifts your heels

And you will fly
Up overhead
But then wake up
And be in bed

But no more dreams
And no more flying
As I lie in my bed
And begin crying

But now it's over
I dream with warning
That I disapprove
And so I'm mourning.

Nicolas Petersen-Gyöngyösi (15)
Munich International School, Starnberg, Germany

Hope

Dull and dark,
No beat of the jungle's heart,
Only engines roaring bright,
Making life turn into a fright
Of surviving or death
In the wide range of emptiness.

But in the dark,
A wink of light,
To take away the fright,
To make a home
And give again,
What was withdrawn from them!

Partnerships kindle passion
And more,
Can't take away the sore
Pain inscribed in their heart,
But can be a part
Of keeping this away from others,
And let them live,
Like their fathers and mothers.

Raphaela Baumgartner (14)
Munich International School, Starnberg, Germany

I Have A Dream

A dream is not - a realisation?
An eagle over a bird's nest.
Lethal thorns, thick as blood in sight.
The fear from east to west.
The fright of night, a delight?

What we feel is what we know -
It shines through what we show.
A bullet - hotter as it passes,
The body, cold remains.
The fear - trustworthy,
The security - unreliable.

This is not a dream of contempt,
But a truth of all new hatched eggs.

Jonathan Schiess (16)
Munich International School, Starnberg, Germany

Freedom

Hard to achieve
When so crowded.

Impossible to keep
In a forest so fresh and keen.

Deforestation
Taking upper hand

And nowhere sways
The freedom marching band.

Nico Kerschbaumer (15)
Munich International School, Starnberg, Germany

Solving A Problem

There were three different people
And three different stories.

The optimist was faced with a problem.
He ignored it saying:
'It will be all right; it will be solved.'

The pessimist, too, was faced with the problem.
He ignored it saying:
'It cannot be changed; it cannot be solved.'

The realist was faced with the same problem.
He thought for a while and then said:
'This is serious but I think it can be solved.'

The optimist was happily ignorant.
But then as the problem grew and he started to worry,
It was too late for him.

The pessimist continued on as he had,
Aware of the problem, but thinking there was nothing to be done.
It was too late for him also.

The realist thought about the problem,
And he found a solution, it was solved.

I think that a lot of problems could be solved
If we thought the way the realist did.
A lot of times we think like the other two.
They thought that it could not be solved,
Or that somebody else would do it in their stead.

Be realistic; problems do not solve themselves.

Johanna Liljegren (14)
Murree Christian School, Murree, Pakistan

I Have A Dream 2009 - Global Verses

Where Is The Key?

Where is the key to this world?
The whole world needs it!

Where is the key to this world?
Children hunger and thirst!

Where is the key to this world?
Parents abandon their kids!

Where is the key to this world?
Boys have to go into the army to fight!

Where is the key to this world?
Girls can't go to school and get educated!

Some people have already found the key to this world.
They can love and forgive others.

Some people grasp at that key so they can
Invite the sick and homeless into their houses.

Some people use the key repeatedly so
They can build schools for girls.

Some people who hold the key tightly,
Don't start fights or war.

Some people who have the key to this world,
Really try their hardest to bring peace that will last.

Where is the key to the rest of this world?
Please, someone help this world find the key!

Karuna Detsch (13)
Murree Christian School, Murree, Pakistan

Judge Me Not

I try to do right,
I make mistakes,
I don't want to fail,
I can't find the brakes.

Some things happen
We can't change,
It happened to me,
My life rearranged.

To something different,
The truth be told,
I try to do better,
I do what I'm told.

This day I failed,
I didn't try hard,
I'm a bad person,
I let down my guard.

Blame me, blame me,
It's all my fault,
I can't change this now,
Not in this world.

I am doing better,
I don't make mistakes,
My grades are getting higher,
I passed 1st grade.

Mariana Chugg (13)
Murree Christian School, Murree, Pakistan

A Peaceful World

A dream in which the world is in peace,
To make all Earth's problems cease.
No more violence and no more pain,
To bring relief like the African rain.

No more violence and no more war,
To bring peace out of the human core.
The destruction of things will end in a dream,
To push off the rain and let the sun gleam.

A peaceful world without fears and tears,
No more drinking and no more beers.
No more pain, yes peace is winning,
No more evil and no more sinning.

The darkness of the world will flee,
Beauty will be the only thing we see.
Evil will be gone forever,
We will never see evil again, no, never.

We have no need to tremble and worry,
We have no reason to be guilty and sorry.
For we will have no pardons to give,
This is the way that we should live.

People will not worry and will not be grim,
People will sing out in a wonderful hymn.
They will have a party and have joy and glee,
They will all be singing in glorious unity.

David Smith (13)
Murree Christian School, Murree, Pakistan

The World We Live In

Happy mothers, children playing, helpful, loving neighbours,
Kitty cats and lily pads and any little favours,
Everybody being friends and no one ever fighting,
No more wars, no famines, droughts, or anything that's frightening.

Is that the world that you would like, the world you'd like to live in?
Is that the world that seems all right, where everything is given?
I think we all would like this world, with peace and joy and love!
I think we all would shine so bright, like stars from up above.

Grieving mothers, children dying, hateful, angry hearts,
Bitterness and mocking, that tear our hearts apart!
Rivers that are full of tears and some that fill with blood,
Wars and famines, droughts and sickness, dying, blooming buds.

This is the world we really live in, this is the sickening truth!
This is the world that we can see; that spoils even our youth!
Is this the world that you would pick, is this what you prefer:
The world that's filled with so much pain
where all these things occur?

If I could change the world, I would, if I could kill the pain!
If I could mend it all, I would, like lovely, cooling rain!
But I can change the world, like lovely, cooling rain!
But I can change the world; I can, in even little ways,
And I will try to change the world, for the rest of my days!

Elin Isaksson (14)
Murree Christian School, Murree, Pakistan

Make A Difference

You can make a difference,
You don't have to be important,
Like Martin Luther King Jr,
Or George Washington,
Or Abe Lincoln,
Or even your class president.

All you need is a good mind,
A strong conscience,
A kind heart,
And a brave spirit.

Get help from others,
There's safety in numbers.
Many people can help more,
Try six, five or four.

You can make a difference,
You don't have to be important,
Like Bill Gates,
Or the President,
Or Winston Churchill,
Or anybody.
Just be yourself.

Jared Armistead (14)
Murree Christian School, Murree, Pakistan

I Have A Dream Of A World That Is Good

You can change the world,
Be someone different, do something new.
Why someone else, why not you?

Why don't you do something new,
Something that few people do?
Be kind to the poor, the homeless and the lame.
If you were them you would want them to do the same.

You can change the world,
Be someone different, do something new,
Why someone else, why not you?

I have a dream of a changed world,
Where there are no problems, where people aren't bad,
Where people are good and where people are glad,
Where there is no violence, no corruption, no hate,
A place where we could all be mates.

You can change the world,
Be someone different, do something new.
Why someone else, why not you?
I think you could, I think you should,
For I have a dream of a world that is good.

James Barker (13)
Murree Christian School, Murree, Pakistan

I Can Change The World

I have a dream, to change the world
To change its culture and some laws,
Since some have died with few flaws.
Persecution and execution,
Both have occurred from religious views.
I can change this just with words.
It might work, it might not,
But I am not the one to decide.
Either my will or not,
God's will should always be done
Even though I am not strong enough,
He alone will give me strength,
Which will be more than enough.
No more fighting, no more wars,
No more loss and no more crying.
How good it will be to see no one flee,
But waiting for the day when we will all be free.
If I believe and pray, then I can really say,
I can change the world.

YoHan Noh (13)
Murree Christian School, Murree, Pakistan

Bringing Us Down

Which way am I going
Up or down?
What things should I change
About my life?
What thing do I do
That brings me down?

Why is it so easy to do the things
That bring me down?
Why is darkness followed by so many
Who go down?
Why do we love the things
That bring us down?

I won't let it be me
Someone who goes down.
I will not go to the one
Who is trying to bring me down.
I know it is hard
But don't go down.

Alex Lehmann (14)
Murree Christian School, Murree, Pakistan

To Make The World Better

If war could end,
And less rare be a friend,

The world might be better.

Less litter dropped,
And fewer animals' lives stopped,
The world might be better.

All you need,
Is a pencil and paper,

To help make the world better.

A pen is mightier than the sword.
That's the word.

Therefore help make the world better.

You have more power than you know,
To tell the world how you think.

It could be better.

Joel Stock (13)
Murree Christian School, Murree, Pakistan

Where There Should Be . . .

Where there should be peace there is
War, endless war, fighting and killing!

Where there should be patience, gentleness and quiet there is
Anger, shouting and madness!

Where there should be happiness and joy there is
Depressing words, sorrow and sadness!

Where there should be laughter, fun and feasts there is
Misery, grief, hunger, dreary minds and souls!

But there is still hope:
People are feeding the homeless!

But there is a glimmer of light:
People do smile at strangers!

But there is still the possibility of peace:
People are laughing with their friends!

Why don't you try to make the difference that you want to see?

Naemi Lanz (13)
Murree Christian School, Murree, Pakistan

War

People cry, tremble and shout madly,
They fight against close friends sadly.

Sometimes they want to stop,
But they can't . . . they must not drop!

Always shouting meaningless words,
Always fighting with sharp, piercing swords.

But if, just they were kind,
Changed hearts they would find.

Pray, just pray, that's all we can do,
Until the war finally ends and pleases you!

HyoJi Song (12)
Murree Christian School, Murree, Pakistan

You Can Change The World

You can change the world, it all started from above.
It is something that we all must be thinking of,
Changes in sadness and improvements in love.

We will all stand on the shoulders of giants.
They have made improvements in science and math,
And for us they have constructed a brand new path.

If you change the world, it will continue to grow.
Things do come and go and they are really not slow.
So before time runs out, get to it! Don't go with the flow!

The world needs improving; it is in dire need.
There are houses to build and homeless to feed.
You think you're not doing well, at least you can read!

If you're not already good, you can change your act.
It changes the world, and that is a fact!
The smallest thing helps the world get uncurled.
Just remember, you can change the world!

Michael Kietzman (14)
Murree Christian School, Murree, Pakistan

Words To Change The World

All throughout history,
And all throughout time,
People have said wrong things,
Causing chaos, war and crime.

All the world leaders,
And all the super powers,
With just one single word,
Can bring down even the mightiest of towers.

However not all words are bad,
Some bring love and peace,
Words can change the man,
And cause suffering to cease.

Wise words can change the future,
They can bring new ideas to Man,
Men shall build on the shoulders of others,
Just speak out and believe you can.

Jamie Lannon (13)
Murree Christian School, Murree, Pakistan

I Have A Dream

I have a dream to change the world,
Because throughout life people have quarrelled.
But I always thought I needed more,
To get rid of crime, revenge and war.

I didn't think I could make a difference,
I thought I would be an interference.
I didn't want to get in the way,
But then I found it would be okay.

Through God I can do anything,
I can even be a king.
I can change the world,
And bring peace to those who once quarrelled.

Through Him I can bring peace,
And make smoking and drugs cease.
If it's His will, I can do it,
I can change the world.

Jordan Lunsford (13)
Murree Christian School, Murree, Pakistan

Who Says You Can't?

Who says you have to be a star
Or need an actor's fame?
Who said you need a smart sports car,
To have a known and honoured name?

Whoever said that kids don't count?
Who says they are too small?
To do a thing of great amount;
That all they'll do is fall?

Don't let them stop your race in life,
Your drive to make a change,
You can help in pain and strife,
To clean up, to not derange.

Anyone can change the world,
It could be youths, or seniors too,
To get some of our mess unfurled . . .
That person could be you.

Elizabeth Wiley (14)
Murree Christian School, Murree, Pakistan

Dream

It was cold and damp,
I fell asleep in a golden camp.
Had a dream about a boy,
Who was weak and had no joy.
He had no home or food,
Every day he was in a bad mood.
He always stole and ate wheat curries,
With always a weed of worries.

Woke up and found a boy,
He was poor and had no toy.
I ran to him and gave him some food,
The boy ate the food and was in a good mood.
I said to him to come to my place,
Where there is always a happy face.
I said to him, 'No worries,
We can eat tons of chicken curries!'

Peter Jung (15)
Murree Christian School, Murree, Pakistan

I Have A Dream

I have a dream . . . to eradicate AIDS that steals from us,
Pilfering all the souls that make life exist,
I see the world crying with this bouldering mass,
Heaving with so much weight that people cannot subsist.

Leaders ought to mull this over,
Juggle the possible answers to this problem,
Create a protective cover,
That people can lean on as their stem.

I dream for hope and peace,
With envisions of a mind that can eliminate this prickling virus,
It requires you and I to make changes that will cease
To create a battlefield that will withstand this germ, like a desert cactus.

I see children suffer, while parents mourn,
Struggling to help each other with the little they have,
Others are torn
Between pieces they cannot save.

My dream is to enhance doctors with advancement,
And technology that will track and attack,
In order that AIDS may have a replacement,
Such that ailing victims may bargain their precious lives back.

I dream for professionals
With envisions of creating leaders that prioritise our disruptive state,
What we need is the intelligence of personnel,
One that can preserve the world's future fate.

But I'll tell you what the world needs . .
An acquired knowledge from a successful mind
That will eradicate all its deeds,
And exterminate AIDS in the face of mankind.

I craft my dream into one that can subsequently put smiles on faces,
Give hope to those who lack
And be the ultimate answer to the world's deadliest virus!

Mitlam Teno (17)
Port Moresby International School, Boroko, Papua New Guinea

My Dream, My Passion

I have a dream, a passion for preventing bullying.
Bullying appears anywhere and everywhere,
Not just at school or on the streets.
I want to prevent and help do something about bullying,
I endeavour to help the victims but also the bullies.
I need you to understand a world with no war and no bullying,
A world with peaceful relations for everyone.
A place where everyone is just as kind to an enemy, (as if it were a friend).
Bullying can't stop until we know it is happening;
War cannot end until we gain trust of each other.
Friends cannot be made with hatred in our minds,
And our future is impossible without having friends.

What would the world be like without hatred?
How can we abolish hatred?
What would the world be like without fear?
How can we abolish fear?
What would the world be like without war?
How can we abolish war?
What would the world be like without bullying?
How can we abolish bullying?

When you bully, you are hurting a potential friend.
When you start a war, you are creating enemies.
When you think of hatred, you are creating more hatred.
When you isolate someone, you are isolating someone who
                              could have easily been you.
When you ignore bullying, you are ensuring it remains!

When you see bullying - try to stop it.
When you see bullying - report it.
When you see bullying - try to learn from it.
When you know bullying happens - try to prevent it!
When bullies are petrified
And the innocent have been liberated,
And when friends are made to bolster each other,
Bullying is no longer a threat and . . .
Life is finally pleasurable!

Toby Duckworth (14)
St Francis of Assisi RC Technology College, Aldridge

I May Just Be A Kid But I Can Change The World

Imagine if I was up there
Amongst all the greats:
Martin Luther King,
Gandhi and Bob Geldof,
What a man he is, indeed.
They were all just people
Like you and me,
But then they took a stand
And weren't what you believed.

I may just be a kid,
But I can change the world.

No more violence,
No more racism,
No more judging each other
On appearance or personality.
No more wars,
No more deaths,
No more hating someone you don't know.
That's what I want to see happening
In your world and mine.

I may just be a kid,
But I can change the world.

I want to see some happiness,
Kids dancing on the streets.
I want to see some love,
All men brothers,
And all women sisters.
Let me see some joy!
Let me see some excitement.
Let me hear harmonising laughter
And see all your beautiful smiles.

I may just be a kid,
But I can change the world.

So kids, put down your toys,

Men put down your arms,
Women raise your voices,
But not in alarm.
Make the future bright
For your children and their children,
And so on,
Until the end of time.

I may just be a kid,
But I can change the world.

Megan Danks (14)
St Francis of Assisi RC Technology College, Aldridge

I Have A Dream

I have a dream
Or so it seems
Of oceans so blue
And grass so green
Of enemies that walk hand in hand
And of countries which don't fight over land.

I have a dream
Or so it seems
That poverty stricken countries
Will be put on a support scheme.
They have men shooting and killing
All over the land
For something they don't even understand.

I have a dream
It will all stop one day
And they will return home
And there they will stay.

I have a dream
That this will be
Not a dream
But reality.

Laura Bradley (14)
St Francis of Assisi RC Technology College, Aldridge

I Have A Dream

Racism,
Is it really worth the hate?
The look of despair on the poor man's face,
Eyes filled with fear,
His dark skin trembling.
Is it really worth the hate?
All because he's of different race.

Racism,
Is it really worth the hate?
Screams of anger in the streets,
Names for all those to hear,
Those it is aimed at shed a tear.
This poor man doesn't know what to do,
He's running, hiding, lost in this world of pain.
Is it really worth the hate?
All because he's of different race.

Racism,
Is it really worth the hate?
Too scared to move from out of your house,
Into the bitter world outside.
A gang of youths upon your lawn, waiting for you to bite.
Your kids are upstairs; you don't know what to do,
You want to keep them safe.
Is it really worth the hate?
All because he's of different race.

Racism,
Is it really worth the hate?
He turns up to work and sees the look on your face.
He tries to ignore the whispers conjuring up inside,
Telling him to stand up and fight back for what is right.
He doesn't.
He puts it behind him, hoping your comments will stop.
Is it really worth the hate?
All because he's of different race.

Racism,
Is it really worth the hate?
One day I wish it would cease and wash the screams away.
I have a dream that this human race can live together face to face.
Can we work together and help all those of different race?

Joshua Wood (14)
St Francis of Assisi RC Technology College, Aldridge

I Have A Dream

I have a dream that I want to see,
A world of peace and harmony.
A place where you are not alone,
A place that we can all call home.
A place of joy and fun and care,
A place that we are happy to share.

I have a dream that I want to see,
A world without war or poverty.
A world that we can appreciate,
A world where loves takes over hate,
A world that I have longed to see,
A place of virtue and integrity.

I have a dream that I want to see,
Beautiful trees sway gracefully.
Where flocks of birds soar through the air,
Where horses gallop without a care,
Where stars sparkle in the twilight hour,
Where every hill blossoms a flower.
Where lakes glisten beneath the sun,
Not a single sound of war or a gun.

I have a dream where my message gets through,
Not just in your heads but in your hearts too.
And we feel secure all across the Earth,
So the world is one, for the next birth.

Sophie Gardner
St Francis of Assisi RC Technology College, Aldridge

I Have A Dream . . .

You may say I'm a dreamer,
But I'm just a strong believer.
Love, hope and friendship go a long way,
So ban all evil, that surrounds us every day.

Fairy-tale joys keep us together,
We are as one forever and ever.
Harmony and peace will never fade,
Along with those images and fantasies made.

Rosa Parks, Bob Geldof too,
Have shown us how God's given talents have seen then through.
Spreading peace around the globe,
Let's follow their example . . . and watch a new world evolve.

Nation to nation join hand in hand,
Sharing the world for each woman and man.
Equal rights are at the top of my list,
Abolishing war into a mist.

Family and friends that are always there,
Holding each other's hands through sadness and despair.
Strangers passing on the street,
Soon to become friends you regularly meet.

Loving one another as I have loved you,
Keep flowers blossoming, through and through.
Technology and inventions fly away with the wind,
Leaving Man to live in peace with all living things.

I have a dream . . .
I hope you do too,
We can all be dreamers together,
And make it come true.

Shannon MacLellan
St Francis of Assisi RC Technology College, Aldridge

If The World . . .

If the world had a voice,
What would it say?
Would it try and scream
All our hatred away?

If the world had eyes,
What would it see?
Would it see people caged,
Trying to break free?

If the world had ears,
What would it hear?
Would it hear orphaned children
Crying in fear?

If the world had a voice
I wish it would cheer
And sing songs of joy
Year after year.

If the world had eyes
I wish they would see,
Every country and nation
In perfect unity.

If the world had ears
I wish the only sounds
Would be laughing, cheering,
And dancing around.

If the world was like this,
I know we would be
Amazingly happy,
I know, you'll see.

Georgia Blunt
St Francis of Assisi RC Technology College, Aldridge

I Have A Dream

I have a dream,
Imagine a world without any criminals,
Imagine a world without any crimes,
Well don't imagine, make it happen,
Be the dream. Utopia will come!

I have a dream,
A place where there are cures for illnesses,
A place where global warming has stopped,
A place where we all work together, make it happen,
Be the dream. Utopia will come!

I have a dream,
To beat all bullies and stop racism,
To beat all bullies and say no,
To beat all bullies we have to work together, make it happen,
Be the dream. Utopia will come!

I have a dream,
Streets become safe streets,
Streets become friendly streets,
Streets become free and clean of harm,
We need to work together, make it happen.
Be the dream. Utopia will come!

I have a dream,
We will all work together to make it happen,
To make my dream become a reality.
Be the dream. Utopia will come!
Be the dream now!

Shannon Williamson (13)
St Francis of Assisi RC Technology College, Aldridge

You Are The Dream!

Since a little girl, I dreamed to grow up
In a world with no violence and no hatred.
But as I grew up, I learnt
That the world was a much different place . . .

It was a world with violence, war and racism.
It was not the world I imagined.
But together we can be the candle of hope and truth
And wash away the darkness of evil.
We are the children of a colour-blind God
And together we can change the world.
Become the love, be the fire in our hearts,
Don't say it, do it.
Stop, stand, speak, carpe diem and believe!

We will stand up, we will believe and
We will change the world!
Without us there is no world,
Without us there is no love,
And without us there is no future.
Become the light in our darkness!

I still have this dream and one day,
If we all stand up and believe,
We can make this dream come true.
We can make the perfect Utopia, and remember . . .
You are the dream.

Gemma Lacey (13)
St Francis of Assisi RC Technology College, Aldridge

I Have A Dream

Dreams, ambitions, targets and goals,
Everybody has these, for without dreams
Our lives would come to a halt.
Some set out to accomplish their dreams,
Some don't.
Some just linger and continue to dream,
Whilst others stand back and refuse to be involved.

The world is the limit, as far as dreams go,
But the world can fight back,
And accomplishing dreams halts to a toll.
People lose faith,
Think that their dreams can't become real,
And then they finally give up.

Dreams are fantasy,
However they can become real.
All you need is a touch of faith and hope,
And be prepared to face your fears.
This has happened in the past,
And is sure to happen not far from here.
People who set out to accomplish their dreams,
No matter what's to fear.

I have a dream
That with a little hope,
We can all stand strong, and never give up.

Henry Bath (14)
St Francis of Assisi RC Technology College, Aldridge

Dare To Dream?

I believe in a better world,
A kinder world,
A safer world,
A stronger world,
Do you dare to dream?

I believe in a free world
Not a nightmare of war.
A dream of love,
No gunfire, no murder, no violence.
Do you dare to dream?

I believe in a vision of love,
A non-abusive world,
A non-prejudiced world.
Do you dare to dream?

I believe in carpe diem,
A world with no illnesses,
Not a world where you are attacked on your own street.
Do you dare to dream?

Do you dare to dream?
Live in Utopia.
Do you believe in a free world
A world with hope?
Do you dare to dream?

Alex Henley (12)
St Francis of Assisi RC Technology College, Aldridge

I Have A Dream . . . My Dream

I have a dream that one day the world
Will be able to sleep without the worry of war,
Hunger, terrorism, famine and disease.
I have a dream that one day the world
Will be able to sleep with the feeling of security
And won't have to worry about discrimination,
No matter what colour, religion or ethnicity.

I have a dream that I will be able to help
Make these changes with information
We have gleaned from the past.
I have a dream that I will be satisfied with life
And what I have accomplished, and to know
I have made a real difference,
Even if it is to just one person.

To achieve these things the world must understand
That there is no achievement with no effort,
There is no satisfaction with no dignity
And there is no pride with no honesty.

The world needs to learn not to dwell
On the past and hold grudges, but to
Concentrate on the future because soon that
Will be the past and we don't want to dwell on that.

Thomas Bannister (14)
St Francis of Assisi RC Technology College, Aldridge

I Have A Dream

I had a dream, magnificent,
Of things I long to see.
A peaceful world, equality.
No warring or poverty.

I started to stir, my dream less clear,
Some children afraid and in despair.
A witness to fighting, torture and death,
I was feeling cold and alone.

I want my dreams, magnificent,
It's not impossible to achieve.
Alive, awake, people living in harmony.
It's something I can see.

Hear this! Join together; let us be as one.
Touch hearts, lean out to one another,
Leave the past with hatred, greed and disrespect.
Tomorrow's the future, step along with me.
Leave fear behind.

Let's live together,
Help me sow the seed,
I have a magnificent dream.

Harriet Quigley (14)
St Francis of Assisi RC Technology College, Aldridge

I Have A Dream

I have a dream
Inspired by sights I've seen.
A dream of peace and love,
And faith in the God above.

I have a wish,
That hate and death will finish.
Fighting will stop forever,
So we can live as one forever.

I have an expectation,
That people will end deforestation.
So that birds and bees,
May live freely as they please.

I have a plan,
Regarding things we should ban,
So that people can see,
It's possible for the world to live in harmony.

So I ask you today,
Do you agree it's okay?
To take, kill and fight,
Is that really what's right?

Eve Chambers (14)
St Francis of Assisi RC Technology College, Aldridge

My Dream

My dream is of a peaceful place
Away from all other sounds
But for the whistle of the wind in my ears
And the voices of the trees
Who sing in perfect harmony.

My dream is of a place that's full of care
Where people take the time to stare
At wondrous waters and magnificent mountains
That fill the land with life and joy
For us who take the time to look.

My dream is of a sunlit sea
Where waves crash so gracefully
Upon the sandy shores on which I stand
Still as I can be
Where I breathe in the air of peace.

My dream is one which I believe
Is how the world is meant to be
Free from fear, anguish and hate
Filled with joy and care and love
And that is my dream.

Cammeron Meades (14)
St Francis of Assisi RC Technology College, Aldridge

Can You Imagine?

Can you imagine . . .
A world without violence?
A world where everyone is safe from the danger of drugs?
A world where the concept of global warming is forgotten?
Where everyone who lives in poverty will have love and safety?

Do you dare to dream, to imagine this world
Without discrimination, child abuse and war?
This is the time, the time to live out our dreams!
This is the time to go forth and conquer!
Live out your life as you should!

God, we are your children, listen to our prayers,
We are united as one, we have one voice
And we all follow a single dream,
The dream that one day this world will rise above its reprobates
And have our freedom to love one another.

Now is the time, but time is running out.
Will you let this ticking bomb blow up
And crush your dreams?
Will you act now or later?
It's up to you!

Jake Heaney (13)
St Francis of Assisi RC Technology College, Aldridge

I Have A Dream

One day,
This world will grow up,
It will thrive, blooming,
Just like the roses in spring,
Beaming, bright and beautiful.
Birds will chirp and chant,
To the sound of song.
While your ears relax,
To harmonious melodies.

What is the damage in that?

One day,
There will be no need for sighs,
Only upbeat, jubilant laughter.
There will be no anger or sorrow,
But awe at wonders of mankind.
There will be no need to fight
But tranquillity everywhere.
Let there be world peace.
That's my paradise, my dream,

What is the damage in that?

Mei Pang (14)
St Francis of Assisi RC Technology College, Aldridge

Speak And Utopia Will Come

If we speak for others,
Utopia will come.
If we do not fight,
Utopia will come.
If we treat others as we would like to be treated,
Utopia will come.
If we work to find cures for cancer,
Utopia will come.
If we stop or even end the wars,
Utopia will come.
If we remember our brothers and sisters
Around the world,
And treat them with equal respect,
Utopia will come today.
If we work now instead of later,
Utopia will come.
If we dream, Utopia will not come.
But if we act and only do right,
Utopia will come.
Together we can do this,
We can make Utopia come.

Daniel D'Arcy (13)
St Francis of Assisi RC Technology College, Aldridge

I Have A Dream 2009 - Global Verses

Together We Can

Just think . . .
At night children lay their heads
Somewhere they are not safe.
We can change this.
Don't let anyone say you can't, because together we can.

Just think . . .
A safe world is out there waiting,
Where there is no war but peace, Utopia.
We can make this,
Don't let anyone say you can't, because together we can.

Just think . . .
The new generation have the intelligence,
Cure for illnesses, renewable energy,
We can create this,
Don't let anyone say you can't, because together we can.

Believe in the future and believe in yourself,
Nothing is impossible,
Don't let anyone tell you different.

Lucy Myatt (13)
St Francis of Assisi RC Technology College, Aldridge

I Have A Dream, I Want To Gleam!

I have a dream to confess,
I want to end the stress,
I want poverty to end,
And I need a hand to mend,
This mess!

I have a dream to
Fly like a bird
And see the world!
And destroy the darkness
And bring the happiness.

Shannan Price (12)
St Francis of Assisi RC Technology College, Aldridge

I Have A Dream!

I have a dream
That there will be a day
When the disease and poverty-stricken
Country of Africa
Will be an oasis of people free from hunger and exile.

I have a dream
That one day our nation
Will be one of peace, love and safety
And not one of violence and despair.

I have a dream
That this nation will soon
Be a Utopia of happiness,
Not from material possessions but from
Living in a world full of joy and equality.

If you have a dream,
It is your job to make it a reality,
So stand up and believe in yourself,
Because I believe everyone's dreams can come true.

Paige Meakin-Richards (13)
St Francis of Assisi RC Technology College, Aldridge

I Have A Dream

I have a dream, a song to sing,
I have a dream that there's no illness and crime.
I would die for everyone to have a home and food.
This is my dream,
That no one is ever unhappy,
People you love and adore will never die,
A world that will never end,
I dream that everyone has a happy life.
Please no battles and dangerous weapons.
I believe that my dream will come true.

Jessica Pridey (11)
St Francis of Assisi RC Technology College, Aldridge

I Have A Dream

I have a dream
To help me through reality
I have a dream
To help the poor
I have a dream
To help them through reality

I have a dream
We can cope with anything
I have a dream
Everyone will be educated
I have a dream
To help those in need

I have a dream
My dream
Will become reality
I have a dream, reality
Will one day be
Just a bad dream.

Phoebe Mas-Griffin (12)
St Francis of Assisi RC Technology College, Aldridge

We Are The Future

One day we wish to live in a world without racism,
Without poverty, in peace and unity with
The rest of the world.
The change should happen and it should be now!
We will help everyone who is stuck in poverty and war
So we can live in a peaceful world!
The change should happen and it should be now!
We are the future, so stand up and speak up
And the change will be now!

Haydon Delaney (13)
St Francis of Assisi RC Technology College, Aldridge

I Have A Dream

My wish is for the world to be in the presence of no fear.
To enable us to look out to space around us
And in our vision to see tolerant people of all cultures bonding.

The dream for people to retrieve forgiveness
And to filter out anguish to become a better person.

The dream of people to contain warm hearts,
Then to naturally give others confidence and
Support on their weaknesses.

Does our world involve hate and not love?
Does our world involve people that take advantage
And do not appreciate?

To fulfil my dream, the world needs to have an aim
To develop a sense of peace.
Leaving a world with no bitterness,
No violence,
Creating a loving community.

Stephanie Westley (14)
St Francis of Assisi RC Technology College, Aldridge

Make Your Dreams A Reality

Our world is engulfed in violence and sorrow,
Discrimination and pain, but together
We can vanquish these serious problems.
This is my fantasy, my dream
That will one day become a reality.
We all stand here with no fear of the outside world
But some are victims of attack because they are black,
Or their ginger hair is curled.
But now we see hope, now we may cope
With the horrors of the world
Because a man named Barrack is unafraid of attack
And the bright future of the world will unfold.

Luke Murphy (13)
St Francis of Assisi RC Technology College, Aldridge

I Have A Dream

I have dreams, too many,
That poor people may have much more than a penny,
That everyone is free of crime
And that all songs have to rhyme,
That all things are as sweet as honey,
And that a silly man never invented money!
That all men at war are at peace with one another,
Because after all every one of them is your brother,
That old people can sleep well at night,
And that scary animals don't bite.
That all blind people can see,
As clearly as me.
That there is much more,
Hero galore.
Dreams, I only have a few,
But I wish each and every one of them may one day come true!

Paige Somers
St Francis of Assisi RC Technology College, Aldridge

I Have A Dream

I have a dream
To help the poor,
Giving everyone equal rights,
Helping the future become bright,
No one can be the best,
No one is better than the rest.

I have a dream
To help the world
Become a better place,
No worries or hard times,
Feeling free every day,
No one can be the best,
No one is better than the rest.

Melissa Peplow (12)
St Francis of Assisi RC Technology College, Aldridge

We Are The Future

We are the past,
We are the present,
We are peacemakers,
We are the basic needs.
We are the hope
We are the future.

We are the answers,
The answers to the world's problems.
We will be united,
United as one.
We will be a unique world,
Everyone will be equal,
Everyone will be the same.
We will jump the obstacles together,
Together we will be the future!

Sophie Lowe (13)
St Francis of Assisi RC Technology College, Aldridge

We Are The Change

Stand up and speak your dreams,
Believe in a better future.
Ignore the word 'impossible'
And take a chance to change the world.

Be the light, be the shepherd, be the change.
Others will follow if you dare to dream,
So see, live and be the better future.

Now is the time to make it happen.
We are the vision of the future.
This is your chance to change the world.
So dream and miracles will happen.
We are the dream and together we are the change!

Eden Beirne (13)
St Francis of Assisi RC Technology College, Aldridge

Footprints In The Sand

Footprints in the sand,
Standing proud and tall,
Watching dreams go by,
Watching them flourish and fall.

Imagine a dream,
That's all you need to do,
A perfect world is out there,
All peacefully and beautifully new.

The time is now to make a difference,
The time is now to change,
It doesn't sound like reality,
It sounds a little strange.

All we need to see
Is our footprints in the sand.

Claudia Pocrnic (12)
St Francis of Assisi RC Technology College, Aldridge

I Have A Dream

I have a dream that everyone can eat,
To feed all families,
To see the poor smile because they are eating,
I have a dream that there is no hunger in the world,
That people who are poor have money,
And can buy things like clean, fresh water!
I have a dream that people in the world do not die,
Because they are starving or dying of thirst,
I have a dream that God is next to them every step of the way,
To help them get through and know that God is
Like an angel next to them,
Could my dream come true?

Chantelle-Rose Hodges (12)
St Francis of Assisi RC Technology College, Aldridge

I Have A Dream

The dawn of civilisation
Was the dawn of war,
Of discrimination,
Of retaliation.
When we were made,
Hammered into creation,
If there is some
God-like one,
Then they made a mistake.

I have a dream
We will fix those mistakes,
Take whatever it takes,
Rake the lice
And mice
In our hair.
The corrupted
And
The erupted ones
Flooded of stupidity,
Blooded of monarchy.

It's time
To rhyme,
To file
The sword.
To line up
The horde
Of the evil lord.

Take them out
With the rake
And make
Justice.

Daniel Claudio Bach Anzolini (13)
St George's College, Buenos Aires, Argentina

What If . . . ?

What if . . .
Both black and white boys
Would play together
Whatever their skin colour might be?

What if . . .
Soldiers, sailors and politicians
Would stop fighting
Only to enjoy life and love?

What if . . .
Pollution would stop, only to see
Polar bears in Antarctica and
White tigers in India living freely?

What if . . .
All those men who died in wars
Would now have great-grandsons
Who told young boys how their ancestors were?

What if . . .
None of those great feelings we have
When something great happens to us
Existed?

What if . . . ?

Tomas Fohrig (13)
St George's College, Buenos Aires, Argentina

I Only Want

(Dedicated to all the children who participated in this competition to change our future. Let's all work together, good luck!)

I only want
Our mighty Earth to be loved, respected,
Our animals, our blue skies, our nature.
I only want a future for my children,
For them to see what we see every day,
What you saw one day.

I only want
To see us acting as a loving family,
As a team, working for a grand objective,
It's our future we are gambling with,
Our lives.

I only want
Our Mother Earth to be revered with passion,
That all living creatures come together,
All animals having a place to peacefully live,
And we humans let them be.

I only want
A world where we are not
Our greatest fear.

Santiago Giovannetti (12) & Pedro Landin (13)
St George's College, Buenos Aires, Argentina

Argentina

Argentina,
The best country on Earth.
Argentina,
Its football amazes the press.
Argentina,
It lifts your spirit when you are depressed.

In the Patagonian Andes we have Bariloche,
With Nahuel Huapi and Nahuelito.
It attracts many people.
In the north we have Jujuy,
With the cerro de los siete colores,
Will inspire a lot of visitors.

Argentina,
We are not number one in sports,
But our crowd will not stop cheering,
Even if we have lost.

So this is why I say,
Argentina, the best country on Earth.

Justo Scherianz & Joaquin Rabuffetti (13)
St George's College, Buenos Aires, Argentina

I Have A Dream

I have a dream
That all children of the world
Can have their parents' love.

I have a dream
That all children of the world
Can grow without fear of being killed.

Because I'm a child
I have the freedom to dream
And not lose my hope . . .

Because I have hope,
I know that the war will stop
And the peace will last forever.

I have a dream
That all the children of the world
Can fulfil their wishes of love!

I have a dream today . . .

Francisco Bottero (12)
St George's College, Buenos Aires, Argentina

Diversity

Diversity is very important,
It's all over the world.
There are different men and women,
And different boys and girls.

Although black and white people
Are always fighting each other,
They can put aside their differences
And stand side by side like brothers.

If people weren't different,
Just imagine the world: very stressed!
All of them would look the same;
It would be boring, dull and colourless.

It's good that diversity exists.
Differences sometimes help us to make friends.
I hope no one fights any more
And that, if the end comes, it's a happy end!

Azul Galo (12)
St George's College, Buenos Aires, Argentina

It Should Not, It Could Not, It Will Not

Nobody's personal traits include perfection
The biggest thing inside of us is fear
We can't always control our anger
That should not stop the butterflies from soaring
That should not stop our hearts either
Sometimes we think that our outsides
Are more important than our insides
Sometimes we let little worries stop us from dreaming
Sometimes we get too lazy to get out of bed
That could not stop the leaves from changing every season
That could not stop our hearts either
We can't always tell the difference between right and wrong
We are the big reason for global warming
We sometimes think more of material things than anything else
That will not stop the waves in the ocean from hitting the shore
That will not stop our hearts either.

Julianna Clark (13)
St George's College, Buenos Aires, Argentina

I Have A Dream

'It was a library where I first saw her',
It's frustrating.
The first line of a novel goes nowhere,
Your mind filled with an empty, blank space.

Your fingers tremble and your stomach aches,
Your mind longs for more as you turn page after page,
Your thoughts clouded, walls cluttered,
Everything is covered by a blanket of dark residue.

It's funny,
Everyone writes about fame and fortune,
No one speaks for the Little Man
Or the one that aches beyond the hospital window
Or the grey skies.

They deserve more than this, than that,
Than the clouded dreams,
A dirty ashtray and empty wine bottles.

And the novel continues, 'I might like you . . .'

I think the stars long for freedom,
Just as restless as the Little Man.
Our dreams can bring us beyond imagination,
Our fate is in the hands of our actions.
What you think is laid upon familiarity.

There is a confusing, constant, cluttered darkness,
But beyond that is eternal sunshine.
If you look hard
Outside these cluttered walls,
The heaven's out there awaiting you.

I have a dream.

Erin McEvoy (14)
St Louis Grammar School, Kilkeel

Dreaming

As I look at the clock,
It's getting close to ten.
Thoughts are running through my head,
It's that time again.
Will I be able to close my eyes?
I'm too afraid to sleep.
Dreams can turn against you,
Images in my head to keep.

Once I had this crazy dream,
It started off so well,
I had everything I ever wanted,
But then my life turned to hell.
I blinked just once,
That's all it took.
Everyone was different,
I couldn't bear to look.

My friends were turning against me,
Had I done something wrong?
I was just trying to be myself,
Hadn't felt so empty in so long.
They said I was acting too mature,
But is growing up such a crime?
Just because I was different from them,
Everyone has to at some time.

Was I actually dreaming?
I'm really not quite sure.
Sometimes my dreams feel so alive,
I wonder if there's a cure.
Thoughts entwining in mind,
Your dreams can be so real,
Playing back memories in your head,
This is when you show how you truly feel.

Jessica Amy Leggett (14)
Sawtry Community College, Huntingdon

The Dream

A man is walking down a street,
I watch the rhythm of his feet.
His ugly face keeps most away,
But he is who I seek today.

His dark brown eyes flit to and fro,
He's looking for someone he doesn't know.
This man foresees that death will come,
The lifeless corpse he will become.

His paranoia deep inside
Is caused by a dream he had last night.
The end is near, he knows for sure,
But it will be quick - no blood, no gore.

A truck comes streaking down the road,
Spilling the contents of its load.
The driver has lost control,
Survival is his only goal.

The man still stands on the edge of the street
Waiting for his final heartbeat.
You cannot understand or even see
That poor man, well he is me.

Sam Brooks (12)
Sawtry Community College, Huntingdon

I Had A Dream

I had a dream
And I hope it comes true.
It was a lovely dream
Of the people I love,
My mum and dad, my nan and grandad,
All of my sisters and my dog,
On our holiday, having fun
In the sun, on the beach,
In the park, at the arcade
Until it was dark.
Then to bed, to dream away.
I couldn't wait until the next day.

Phoebe Avenell (12)
Sawtry Community College, Huntingdon

Your Future

Can you see your future
Clear in your head?
Will you live in a different culture
Or stay at home in bed?

Leave school early
Or stay on till the end?
Change your look completely
To look just like your friend?

Find the perfect job
Or forever stay at home?
Finally learn to cook on the hob
Or order takeaways by phone?

Your dream is yours to find,
Your dream is yours to live.
Follow your dream, your future,
Even if you don't know what it is.

Natasha Skinner
The Castle School, Bristol

Dream

Picture this,
A world with no wars.
Picture this,
With no broken laws.
Picture this,
Where stars shine so bright.
Picture this,
All through the night.
Picture this,
Where there's no use for a pill.
Picture this,
Because nobody's ill.
Picture this,
Where there's no global warming.
Picture this,
Because a new age is dawning.
Picture this,
Where everyone's excited.
Picture this,
And a new candle's lighted.
Picture this,
It burns through the night.
Picture this,
A blinding light.
Remember this poem
And always be keen
To keep this in mind
As it is my dream!

Alex Haigh
The Castle School, Bristol

If I Ruled The World
(An excerpt)

If I ruled the world,
Animals would roam free
And birds would sing in every tree.

If I ruled the world,
Plants could grow where they wanted
And insects would leave people alone.

If I ruled the world,
The trees would stand where they stand today
And the rainforests would be left untouched.

If I ruled the world,
The flowers would be left to grow on their own
And rare ones would be left in their native habitat.

If I ruled the world,
Petrol would be eco-friendly
And people would cycle to work.

If I ruled the world,
Everyone would have the chance to go to school
And on to university.

If I ruled the world,
People would grow crops in exchange for money
And no one would live in poverty.

If I ruled the world,
Endangered animals would be part of breeding programmes
And poaching would be banished.

If I ruled the world,
People would grow their own fruit 'n' veg,
And import the rest through trading.

If I ruled the world,
Smoking would become illegal
And all leftover cigarettes would be destroyed.

If I ruled the world,
Everyone would have access to medical care
And most of it would be free.

If I ruled the world,
Hospitals would be clean places to be in
And the food would taste just right.

If I ruled the world,
People could marry who they liked
And wherever they wanted to.

Rachel Spencer (13)
The Castle School, Bristol

Imagine

Imagine a dream.
Imagine
All eyes on her.
Imagine
Stroke by stroke.
Imagine
The end getting closer and closer.
Imagine
Succeeding in her dream.
Imagine
All those happy faces.
Imagine
She is the shining star.
Imagine
That gold medal.
Imagine
The crowd screaming her name.
Imagine
The future, what would it be like?
Imagine
Touching the finishing line.
Imagine
Winning!

Rosanna Pearce (13)
The Castle School, Bristol

Hopes Of A Sheep

Aaahhhhh . . .
Munch!
Lovely spring leaves, fresh and sweet,
Chew!
Leaping through the meadow, light as a lamb.
Swallow!
Grazing the yellow grass, *munch, munch, munch.*
Munch!
Playing with baby sheep, new and barely fluffy.
Chew!
Losing all the wool, growing it back.
Swallow!

Rolling in the snow, sheltering from the rain, relaxing in the sun,
Munch!
Friends with the sheepdog running in the field
Chew!
Silly sheeplings stealing secluded shrubbery.
Swallow!
Leading the way to a new age of sheepism,
What a lovely life it would be!
Baaa!

Tom Bedford (13)
The Castle School, Bristol

A Patchwork Of Dreams

A patchwork of dreams
Sewn together at the seams.
A life of hope
Stored carefully away.
Waiting in the dark,
Afraid to leave their mark.
Collecting dust
As time stands still.
Like Romeo and Juliet
Before they met
Life seeming pointless,
Not worth living at all.
If only they could show
Themselves to the world,
Somehow,
Someday,
They are waiting.
A patchwork of dreams
Coming apart at the seams.
In the dark too long,
Afraid to be themselves.

Emily Craig (13)
The Castle School, Bristol

Imagine

Imagine, in a parallel universe
The sky was orange like mango flesh
And the grass was blood-red.

Imagine, in a parallel universe
Concrete was always sparkling white,
Like a fresh, clean piece of paper.

Imagine, in a parallel universe
Worms lived in trees
And birds pecked holes in the ground.

Imagine, in a parallel universe
Snow wasn't white, but black,
Black as the darkest midnight.

Imagine, in a parallel universe
Where spiders were considered cute
And butterflies as ugly as a dogfish.

Imagine, in a parallel universe
Where everyone lived in peace and harmony,
Like a perfect world . . .

Nicky Moffat
The Castle School, Bristol

Untitled

Imagine
A world with no fighting.
Imagine
If all countries joined together.
Imagine
If all sadness was replaced with joy.
Imagine
Having a house on the moon.
Imagine
If everyone had a fair life.
Imagine
No criminals, no wars and no bad thoughts.
Imagine,
World peace!

Luke Williams
The Castle School, Bristol

Grab Life With Two Hands

We think every day of thing we would love to be:
Famous sports players, athletes, singers,
Knighthoods, we all want them.
I bet your parents say, 'Only the best do that for a living.'
It gets you down.
Well, if you want something so badly,
You would try and be determined
And give maximum effort.
All the famous superstars that we aspire to be
Started from where you are now - at the bottom of the ladder of life.
They worked hard to be where they are now,
They had the edge, the inspiration
And the raw determination to succeed.

Max Hitchcock (13)
The Castle School, Bristol

Imagine

Imagine
One voice in a crowd.
Imagine
Getting your opinion heard.
Imagine
Walking through the streets and getting noticed.
Imagine
Playing music people like.
Imagine
Having your face on CD covers.
Imagine
Hitting the drums until the sticks splinter,
The light's on you.

James Cook (13)
The Castle School, Bristol

Psychiatry

To read someone's mind
What would I find?
Hopes and fears,
Love and tears,
Loss and pain,
Or moral gain?
Depression,
Obsession,
Aggression,
Compulsion,
Disorder?
What would I find?
What will I find?

Jacob Fox (13)
The Castle School, Bristol

Riddell And Mikki's Poem

When I think about my dream,
Happiness springs to mind.
The whole world is one big team,
Be fair and very kind.

Millions of people around the world
Die for no good reason.
Even children are viciously hurled
Into death, why don't you just leave 'em?

If just one person changes their mind,
It will make me very happy.
The whole community will bind,
Even a baby in a nappy.

Mikki Storton & Riddell Erridge
The Castle School, Bristol

My Dream

Smashing every shuttlecock,
Serving short and long,
Today I won some matches,
Tomorrow I'll win some more.
Maybe in a couple of years
I'll be winning medals,
With the pressure pounding me
Like a million pedals.
But now I'm starting to wither,
My winning streak's gone to none,
I'm getting way too old for this,
My dream is over and done.

Matt Roberts
The Castle School, Bristol

Imagine

Imagine . . .
If all hatred turned to harmony,
If all sadness turned to joy.
Imagine . . .
Everybody fit and healthy,
Everybody has no cares or worries.
Imagine . . .
A world where words mean more than violence,
A world where the word 'war' is not in the dictionary.
Imagine . . .
A peaceful world.

Jonathan Witter (13)
The Castle School, Bristol

Inspiration

I n the future I'd like to
N egotiate politics with an MP
S wim the English Channel
P ay off everyone's debts
I nvent a new piece of technology
R un a marathon, give money to charity
A ssociate with terrorists, to help the police
T ravel the world
I dentify a new animal
O ffer £100 to every person on the street
N avigate for a lorry driver.

Sophie Vaughan-Williams (13)
The Castle School, Bristol

Untitled

One dream,
To play before the crowd,
To hear the roar as we come out,
To feel the adrenaline pumping through my body,
To see the oval ball soar into the sky,
To play in the game of the year,
To be next to the ref as he puts his whistle to his mouth,
To hear the loud chirp of the whistle,
That signals the battle to commence.
One dream.

Archie Stenning
The Castle School, Bristol

I Dream

I dream for the future world,
I dream for the generations to come.
I pity them,
I cry for them
Because I am scared about
What they might have to suffer.
I worry that life might not be interesting -
Machines to do everything for them;
That they'll not be able to experience
The small wonder of preparing
Dinner for their dad,
Flipping through a dictionary,
Picking some flowers -
All of those small wonders.

We think we're changing for the best -
But is this really the price we must pay
In return for medicines and treatments?
Is it the only way?

Alexandra Ridley (12)
The European School, Heredia, Costa Rica

Thinking About The World

All these promises,
They are just words,
You actually have to do them
And be concerned.

Think of the animals,
What have they done?
They don't deserve this,
I want the world as one.

What about the environment
And all the litter?
We need to clean up our act
And make the world glitter.

Think of the fishes
Trying to flee
From the horrible black oil
We dump in the sea.

I want to turn the clock back
To those peaceful days,
No war, no cruelty
And no dismay.

Every day I think and wonder
Will the world change
And not let people
Die of hunger?

Now is the time
For us to do our bit,
Now is the time
To do something about it!

Think of the future
And what it might hold,
You have to do something about it
Before you get too old!

Emily Upton (12)
The Read School, Selby

My Dreams

Dreams are usually all about
Beauty and fantasy,
With castles and fairies and unicorns,
Or explorers on the sea.
But my dreams are more serious . . .

My dreams are about
White judging black,
Animals dying down,
And bullies fighting back.

Money going down the drain,
And wars need to stop.
Children are disappearing
And animals getting the chop.

Why is the ice melting?
And why do we have slaves?
Why do people kill people for fun?
And isn't the rainforest something we can save?

The world has become a terrible place;
There must be something we can do.
The world won't care for itself,
So it's up to me and you.

Dreams are usually about
Beauty and fantasy,
With castles and fairies and unicorns,
Or explorers on the sea.
But my dreams are more serious . . .

Bryony Chapman (11)
The Read School, Selby

This Is My Dream

Dreaming about being alone,
No one there to help me.
A strip of light on my face,
No one there to save me.
The drumbeat starts,
Bang! Bang! it goes.
My guitar flies overhead,
Strumming the beat alone.

The microphone crawls up my leg
Then stands in front of me.
What else can I do?
All I can do is sing.
I take a big gulp under my breath,
Then open my mouth and sing.
I sing nothing but the truth,
Which is this,
This is my dream.

I sing along, I start to smile,
All the truth, never a lie.
The last strum of my guitar,
Silence fills the room.
My voice starts to stutter
As I await a reply.
I sing nothing but the truth,
Which is this,
This is my dream.

Molly Browne (14)
The Read School, Selby

I Had A Dream

I had a dream that the Earth would change,
There would be no people,
Only animals would be left on this Earth.

All the buildings would fall down
And rot with mould,
Then all the plants would grow over them,
And disappear under shrubs and trees.
There would not be much shelter
In cruel winters and hot summers.

What would the animals do without humans?
What would they eat?
What could they drink?
Where would they go?

The animals would eat nothing
Except the plants and grass.
They would try and protect their territory
And then fight and kill each other.

They could drink water if it was nearby,
But they may be too weak to travel far,
And without it they would die,
So eventually nothing would be left on Earth.

So, you see, humans and animals do need each other
To exist together, to help change the world,
To make sure it survives!

Nicole Hatton (12)
The Read School, Selby

I Have A Dream

I have a dream
To do my country proud,
To get my country to chant
And get them on my side.

In my dream
All the crowd would stand
And all just for me,
It's all a real big treat.

In my dream
I'm trying to win it,
Win it for my team
And all my country too.

In my dream
I want to do it,
Get the winning runs
To be 'Champions of the World'.

I just remember
Lifting the bat,
The trophy seemed giant,
But it really wasn't that.

Yes, I'm talking about cricket
And won it with the bat,
I did my best
And that really is a fact.

Oscar Sugden (12)
The Read School, Selby

I Had A Dream

I had a dream of a magical land,
Where a suspicious fairy took my hand,
She walked me through the starlit night,
She took me to a place, a wonderful sight.

It was a wonderful world full of life,
A place of happiness, without any strife,
A place where fairy-tale characters stay,
Where it's always a lovely sunny day.

The sky was blue, the grass was green,
The most beautiful place I've ever seen,
A place of joy, of hope and wonder,
Where there's never rain, storms or thunder.

We walked through a meadow full of flowers,
With a cloudless sky, for hours and hours,
We sat in the grass peacefully,
Watching the world around us happily.

But then the worst thing happened to me,
I woke up to see
That in my bedroom there was no meadow,
Just my bed and its dull old shadow.

I realised that the place that I'd just been
Was only a silly little dream,
And I knew that the world would never be the same,
But that would be my lifelong aim.

Megan Backhouse (12)
The Read School, Selby

Excuse Me, Sir

I dream a dream
Walking through the city
The tunnel, the long, dark tunnel
Tab ends infesting the floor
Emerging from the sky
Skyscrapers, flashing lights

Flickering bulbs
A car rushes by
I cross the road, the lonely, quiet road
No one out at this time of night
Except for one man
In the streets he sits at home

'Excuse me!' he cries
I stroll past
The man, the lonely, homeless man
I leave the city
To the outskirts
Almost home

I open the front door
To my home
And there he sits, sits in my chair
I stand gobsmacked
And he says
'Excuse me, Sir.'

Jacob Webster (14)
The Read School, Selby

I Have A Dream . . .

I have a dream to go to a magical land,
Where all the people have soft skin and hands,
All the badness would go away
And all the goodness would have to stay.

In this land there is a queen
Who has the prettiest face you've ever seen.
She wears beautiful gowns and gorgeous pearls,
This will be the world of worlds.

The people will be happy and filled with joy,
Every girl will get that perfect boy.
The families will be happy, with no stress,
In all the houses there will be no mess.

Every summer will be sunny,
Every person will have a daddy and mummy.
In every winter there will be snow,
That is how I want it to go.

So that's my dream, I hope it comes true,
We will all go there, him, me and you.
When we are there we will have such fun,
But now, we wait for that day to come.

Phoebe Simpson (12)
The Read School, Selby

I Have A Dream

I had a dream of fantasy,
I had a dream of symphony,
I had a dream of love,
I had a dream of a beautiful dove.

I had a dream of a magical land,
Where the coast was blessed with pure golden sand.
A fairy came to me and said,
'Come to this land when you lie down in bed.
Come to this land when you're feeling blue,
Making grey skies turn to blue, just for you.'

I had a dream of dew on the ground,
I had a dream of wonder and sound,
I had a dream to change the sad,
To all of the people that are rather bad.

I had a dream that will change the world,
I had a dream that curled and swirled,
I had a dream of the clear blue sea,
I had a dream, a dream just for me.

Brooklyn Kenning (11)
The Read School, Selby

The Millionth Dream

Dreaming again. Yes, I know.
I must dream the best part
Of 65% of a day.
They're not always good.
Death threats - ew.
Sometimes they're good though . . .
Sometimes.
Lock us away then.
Because if we're not allowed to dream,
We might . . . ?

Becca Atkinson (14)
The Read School, Selby

Garden

G arden a little
G arden a lot
G arden in a new garden spot
A dmire a little
A dmire a lot
A dmire the new garden spot
R ush a little
R ush a lot
R ush to see the new garden pot
D ig a little
D ig a lot
D ig in the new garden spot
E ngage a little
E ngage a lot
E ngage with the new garden spot
N ow a little
N ow a lot
N ow the new beautiful old garden pot.

Sophie Thornton (11)
The Read School, Selby

A Perfect World

If all the world was peaceful, with no conflict or wars
If the entire world was free, all open doors
If all living things had eternal life, death would be extinct

If all the world was healthy, with no disease or pain
If all the world was fair, no reason to complain
If all the continents were as one, everyone could learn

If all the world was well fed, no famine and no drought
If all the world was happy, no reason to pout
If all humans were as one, no one would be different.

Andrew Meiklejohn (11)
The Read School, Selby

What Has Happened To The World?

What has happened to the world?
It is dead and alone,
Just a cry from the wind
And a weep from the moon.

What has happened to the world?
Can something be done?
How much longer can it last?
Is it still our home?

What has happened to the world?
It is what we've done
Because we think of us,
This place is not home.

What has happened to the world?
How will I survive?
All these things will happen soon,
So let's start it now!

Eden Batley & Harriet Smith (12)
The Read School, Selby

I Have A Dream

I love to dream of

H olidays, sun and sea
A dventure, to
V enture through the sandy plains and
E njoy a swim in the big, bright sea

A nd escape from school to see the world

D reams are freedom from angry thoughts
R elax in wonderful places
E njoy your dreams
A nd take the time to wish and
M aybe your dream will come true!

Hannah Jolliffe (14)
The Read School, Selby

Look At It!

If you look around,
What do you see?
People dying
And complete misery.

Death is not nice,
We need your help
To save these people,
Can you hear their relative yelp?

Animals that are abused,
It's just not right.
So we need your help
To keep them safe at night.

You wouldn't want it to be you,
So now,
If you help,
Take a big bow!

Lydia Quartley (12)
The Read School, Selby

I Have A Dream

I had a dream,
A very good dream,
A fantasy dream,
A magical dream,
I had a dream.

I had a dream,
A very scary dream,
A mystery dream,
A shocking dream,
I had a dream.

When I had these dreams,
My heart bumped with excitement.
I really wish I could have those dreams again,
I love my drams.

I wonder what will be next!

Martha Veale (12)
The Read School, Selby

I Have A Dream

They say all good things come to an end,
For my grandad thing have just begun.
Although he is not with us anymore,
He has been reunited with my nanny in Heaven.
Every time I think of them
I can now feel a sense of belonging,
Because they have finally found each other
After twenty-one years apart.
So I must not feel sad that he has gone,
And embrace the fact that they are together,
Watching over everyone.
If only I could bring him back from Heaven,
My dream would be complete.

Sam Kavanagh (11)
The Read School, Selby

I Have A Dream

As I lay there,
I dream about you,
Your big, beautiful eyes,
Your long brown hair.
The door opens,
Is it in my dream?
It's in my dream.
My friend is standing there,
Looking straight into my eyes.
Has something bad happened?
Something good?
I don't know.
She starts telling me what has happened,
I don't know what to say.
Why me?
Why are my dreams so confusing?

Hannah Wilson (14)
The Read School, Selby

I Had A Dream

One day I woke up
From the dream I just had,
I had a dream,
It was very extreme.

It took me to a different world,
Different isn't the right word.
I was grown up and tall
And I was driving my family up the wall.

Later on I was lying dead on the street
And I woke up in horror.
I had a dream,
It was more than extreme.

Kashi Nair (14)
The Read School, Selby

I Have A Dream

I have a dream
That in countries there is no war,
So everyone will get along.
Like your children, you don't want
Their children growing up in the war.

I have a dream
That people in wars aren't people with children,
So fathers don't go to war
And risk their lives for people.

I have a dream
That there is no war,
So children don't grow up without their dads.
So think of the people with no dads,
Brothers, grandads or uncles,
Just think before you fight, please.

Laura Metcalf (11)
The Read School, Selby

I Had A Dream

I had a dream
About a world,
It wasn't round,
It was curled!

Dreams are strange,
Dreams are weird,
One of the times
I had a beard!

Once I was an MP,
I claimed for my house,
I claimed for my children's toys
And for their pet mouse!

Harry Campey (13)
The Read School, Selby

I Have A Dream

I have a dream this world will be green,
No more pollution, no more waste.
This world will be green and all over the world
There will be less revs from cars.
I have a dream the cars will be gone,
We'll all be happy to walk.
I have a dream this world is to stay.

Let's all be green and care for this world,
We can stop pollution, we just need to try.
Let's stop the ice caps melting,
Let's all turn to 30°,
'Cause even at 30° it still gets rid of the dirt.
I have a dream we will all be green
And the world won't go.

Jake Stephenson (13)
The Read School, Selby

I Dream . . .

I have a dream
I dream of freedom
I dream of freedom to dream
In which every man, woman or child shall exalt
In the ability to think
To comprehend, desire, understand, envision
In which everyone has the right to be captivated . . .
By a tempest of yearning, a torrent of pictures
A whirlwind of happiness
A land in which people dream of flying elephants,
Or cures to disease, or of peace
In which a whole nation shall stand united
To dream in a channel of symphony
Where every sonic essence of that dream becomes a thread
And a tale of excitement, courage and bravery
Is spun from this thread
Creating an alphabet of dreams
In which people act upon their dreams
Of innocent desires and blissful ignorance -
In which the impossible becomes plausible
The answers to every question answered
Volumes upon volumes of freedom to dream
In which the clocks melt away to the time of Eden
And those with the ability to dream remain
With respect and open-mindedness they charge ahead
Listening to the harmonic dystrophy of dreams -
Clambering away in unison
In one pulsating mass the entire imagination is sparked by fire
Ablaze, yet calm and unnerving
Energetic yet nonplussed
A tower of belief, of strength
We shall respect those with the ability to think different -
To dream
I dream of the freedom to dream.

Akshay Singh Chauhan (15)
United World College of South East Asia, Singapore

Hear The Unheard

My sisters and brothers weep in abandoned silence,
Feverish with hunger and thirst they sit
Waiting for me to take them into my loving arms,
Lighting the candle unlit.

Sleeping on hard cement and eating imaginary rice,
One by one their weakened souls take flight,
Never having seen the things my eyes have witnessed,
Never having realised the difference between morning and night.

While we pull a tantrum, fuss and fight,
Those children, women and men do the same,
But they are fighting for the things we throw,
Their hearts and bodies depend on that game.

Our eyes twitch and fill up with tears,
Some of us don't lack a magnanimous heart,
But it's a message to all those out there,
That action is needed to create a promising start.

Surya Sridhar (16)
United World College of South East Asia, Singapore

I Have A Dream

I have a dream one day global poverty will be no more,
This is a problem no one can ignore.
Children dying daily from starvation,
While kids here play on the PlayStation.
Together we can help these suffering nations,
We can help children that don't have
The simplest forms of medications.
People can't even get simple essentials like water that's clean,
Some children don't live to see nineteen.
So please donate, even if it's as little as a few coins,
And then we can watch the nation as it rejoins.

Ali Hussain (13)
Waverley School, Birmingham

One Day . . .

I know . . .
Sorrow, alone,
So lost and cold.
No house or home,
Still tough as chrome.
No food or money,
Life's no more funny,
The day is dark, the night is darker,
The morning's just a wish,
To never see another again.

If only . . .
People knew, why don't people care?
If only we learnt how to share.
Everyone is equal,
Everyone's the same,
Don't put anyone to shame,
Whether they're famous or not,
If they've got a lot.
There's only one leader,
The leader of us all,
The one who everyone can call.

So why do people get treated differently?
Judged on whether they are rich or poor,
On their looks and more.

The rich are poor and the poor are rich, is what I dream,
How would they feel? Everything's not what it seems.
No luxury, no slaves,
How would they behave?

Poverty's not just the problem
It's made worse by the richer.
An animal is treated with more respect, much more than the poor.
If an animal is hurt, it's taken to the vets' to be cared for,
Why can't we care for people who have nothing there?
They're just like me and you,
So treat them equally too.
They're probably better than us,
Us, who don't appreciate what we do have, but crave for more . . .

The temptation takes us over, the desire,
If someone poor tells the truth they're pointed at as a liar,
Whereas we lie and lie, but everyone believes us,
Just because we're better in status.
What is status but a made-up thing? A division.

The wealthy are fake but seen as real,
The poor are real but seen as fake.
How can the truth be told?
How can it be proved, by making the ground break?

I have a dream one day we'll all be equal, the same,
We won't remember these hard times, when they went or came.

I have a dream no one is rich, neither poor,
However people learn to share more and more.

I have a dream one day there will be no more war,
No more murdering the innocent and spreading more poverty,
This'll be the law.

I have a dream one day my dreams will be true.
I have a dream one day my dreams will be the future,
The better future,
No more inequality, no more war or torture.

I have a dream that my dream will be reality . . .

Sana Sikander (14)
Waverley School, Birmingham

My Dream . . . My Hope . . . My Passion . . .

I hope for a better, brighter future,
Where there's laughter, hope, humour.

I hope there's no neglect,
No war or crime, nothing to protect.

I hope this is published or even a song,
This is all good, nothing wrong.

There's no reason to be afraid,
No guns, no drugs, not even a grenade.

I hope there's no one to break the laws,
Listen to your parents and do your chores.

There's no one who's alone,
There's always someone loving you at home.

I hope there's always a chance of survival,
One slip that could be vital.

I hope the world is always clean,
We can do it if we work as a team!

Little things like catching the bus,
Forget our cars, think of the world and not about us.

Act now, it's time for change,
Living like this, isn't it strange?

I hope there is no danger,
We're all equal, there's no stranger.

This is my hope, my passion, my dream,
One day I wish this will come true.
Stop, wait, think,
Now what can you do?

Faizzan Hussain (14)
Waverley School, Birmingham

You're My Gaza

Gaza, you're worth more than ma fifty-inch plaza,
As I'm listenin' to the news 'bout people dyin',
I try to remember at night while I'm lyin'
The life of mine but what 'bout the others
All those dead sisters and brothers?
Every second of a minute someone dies
Every beat of ma heart someone cries
Those sufferin' the crime can't think about future time
While we're here eating our curry
There are soldiers out there in a hurry
They tryin' everything they can do
Do your bit to help too
Soon will come a time for world war
You won't be hidden behind a closed door
Every time I try to think that there will be equality
I know that it's just a novelty
There are babies out there who have HIV
You could try helping the needy, unity
So stop for a minute
Not try to blink for a minute
In your mind picture the dead
Bone lyin' over bone, covered in red
Let's try to give some charity at least
You're not a tramp so try to make peace
You've got so many credit cards
Your bedroom closets are filled from yards

Give some clothes you don't need
Give them some food to feed
And do a good deed.

Saira Naz (14)
Waverley School, Birmingham

What If?

What if
There was no such thing as cigarettes?
No cravings. No wheezing. No lung cancer.
No children begging their parents to stop.

What if
There was no such thing as drugs?
No addiction. No jail time. No hurt.
No affected families.

What if
There was no such thing as alcohol?
No alcoholics. No pointless fights. No splitting headaches.
No one-minute moments that decide the fate of others.

What if
There was no such thing as bullies?
No name calling. No teasing. No spite.
No innocent people taking their own life.

What if
There was no such thing as poverty?
No crying. No starving. No homelessness.
No children begging on the streets.

Zara Khan (13)
Waverley School, Birmingham

I Wish

I wish that those who are in sorrow
Can wake up happy to see tomorrow.

I wish that people can stand hand in hand,
With peace, harmony and understand.

I wish that those that feel the pain
Can stand up tall and cheer again.

I wish that diseases had a cure
To help everyone, that's for sure.

I wish that blacks and whites will mix,
Instead of turning to punches and kicks.

I wish that orphans had a home,
So they have somewhere and are not alone.

I wish that those, near and far,
Could be proud of who they are.

I wish for wishes every day
And wish my wishes had a say.

One day soon they will come true,
That's a fact I can tell you.

Juma Hussain (14)
Waverley School, Birmingham

Why?

This poem is for those who ask, 'Why?'
For those who say, 'Why can't it be a lie?'
For those who believe in peace and freedom,
Who give up everything for the sake of their people.

All the stealing and the drugs, all the murders and the thugs.
Why? Where's the strength of the people who stick together?
Who say they will fight for the peace forever.

All the people who stand up and say, 'Why?'
Why won't the world change for the better?
We should all stand together for a fight against the rebels.

We'll stand together and do right;
We'll stand together and put up a fight.
We'll stand together so we don't have to question: why?

The world should be a better place for all of us, for every face.
The world will be a better place for all of us,
And there will be no stealing, no drugs, no murders
And definitely no thugs,

All because I fought for what I believe in,
Because we fought for what everyone dreams of.

Ammaarah Arfan (13)
Waverley School, Birmingham

Consider

Consider the world without violence
Consider the world without drugs
Consider being normal then thinking you're a thug
Consider peace!

Consider mortality
Consider humanity
Consider walking down the street without being pointed at
Consider equality!

Consider happiness and joy
Consider immensity of love
Consider the world without war and conflict
Consider sheer bliss!

Consider silence
Consider laughter
Consider enjoyment and harmony
Consider but also hope!

Farhana Ahad (14)
Waverley School, Birmingham

I Have A Dream!

My dreams are stars!
My dreams are fantasies!
My dreams are never-ending!
My dreams are the future!
My dreams are life in picture form!
My dreams are ambitious!
My dreams are music to my ears!
My dreams are an orchestra band!
My dreams are my destiny!
My dreams are hope and joy!
I had a dream!

Jasmine Wood & Keeley Bird (13)
Westley Middle School, Bury St Edmunds

I Have A Dream

A florist shop, all bright and gay,
With marigolds and roses and giant bouquets.
The shop letters say 'Miss Eleanor Trent',
Challenging the opposite shop, crooked and bent.
A graduation letter wrapped in a ribbon to say
I have got into a university.
A bookshop littered with all of my books,
While other authors give me jealous looks.
A bottle of medicine, colourful and bubbly,
Given to the breast cancer charity.
Next to Gucci and Prada displays,
Will be my new designer shop called May.
A brand new fluffy dog and a huge house from
My mum and dad after my big wedding prom.
My husband and I will live a carefree life,
Washed of stress, anger and strife.
Then in my old, old age,
I'll bake cakes and buns and make pies to say
Thank you for such a great time on Earth,
I'll never forget it in any way.

Eleanor Trent (13)
Westley Middle School, Bury St Edmunds

ASC1 Have A Dream

Charlie has a dream that one day there will be no more killing.
Chelsie has a dream that she will become a pop star.
Brendan has a dream to work with Steve Jobs.
Abigail has a dream that she will always be young.
Curtis has a dream that there will be no more wars.
Bartosz has a dream that he will be a teacher.
Katey has a dream that she will become a famous footballer.
William has a dream that he will always make people happy.
We all share the dream that one day we will all be equal.

Class ASC1
West Oaks School, Wetherby

I Had A Dream

I had a dream that I could fly
High up into the sky.
In my dream I could sing like a lark
And my eyes could see in the dark.
In my dream I had three wishes
And one would be to not do dishes.
If I could have three more wishes
I would have a boyfriend called Jake
And spend my life eating cake.
I had a dream I would be an actress
With my pictures in the press.
I wish that I could be an aeroplane
Taking people on holidays, then home again.
In my dream I wished for a slave
To obey the orders that I gave.

Helen Hindle (18)
White Ash School, Oswaldtwistle

All About Me

My hero is me,
The best there can be.
I'm quite good at footy,
But that's just me.

My hero is me,
The best there can be.
Girls think I'm a cutie,
But that's also just me.

My hero is me,
The best there can be.
Right now I look a bit scruffy,
But that's from my parents . . .
Not me!

Sawal Mehrban (14)
Witton Park Business & Enterprise College, Blackburn

Why Be Racist?

I woke up in the morning,
Walking down the road,
Two whites picking on an Asian person,
Calling him words like 'Paki' and 'black'.

Go to school the next day,
Mixed people everywhere.
I look at one side -
A fight.
Two Asians on a white person.
The white person is on the floor,
Tears falling from his bloodshot eyes.
I feel sorry for him.
What can I do?
Tell the teacher?
No, they would just stop them.

What will the world come to?
Can't we just be nice to each other?
Be friends and forgive each other
For our mistakes.

That's why I have written this poem,
To share with everyone,
And one day we will all
Realise our mistakes.
But will we already have
Gone too far to go back?

Ebrahim Patel (12)
Witton Park Business & Enterprise College, Blackburn

I Have A Dream

I have a dream
That war is a myth
And no one was killed,
And that the gun was never made,
Neither the bombs nor grenades.
I knew that the day would never come,
How could I be so dumb?
I want it to be finished and done.

I have a dream
Nobody is supreme
And they don't have to scream,
And when it comes, everyone feels great.
Famine will be defeated
And we'll win the game.

I have a dream,
Picture this scene,
That the world is a better place
Because crime is no more
And people are equal,
Bullying is murdered
And the world is clean.

Liam Greenwood (12) & Sam Parkinson (13)
Witton Park Business & Enterprise College, Blackburn

Jennie

I like Jennie's hair although she looks like a bear.
She is very sound, just like a pound.
She is very nice and she is not that good at catching mice.
She's very kind but she's a bit blind.
She helps me but when I'm bad she belts me.
When I see her smile I run a mile.
There is only one Jennie, there are not many.

Kamran Shah (13)
Witton Park Business & Enterprise College, Blackburn

Isn't It Horrible?

Isn't it horrible, not knowing
What's coming your way?
Whether something good
Or bad will happen.
Whether it will be the best
Or the worst,
When you don't know if you're
Dreaming or actually living it,
Don't know if it's a nightmare
Or you're actually dying.
Isn't it horrible when you can't
Do anything to help
But when it all goes wrong
There's no one to blame but yourself?
This funny, crazy place we live in
Can be good, can be bad,
But when it's coming down to it,
There's nothing it can do,
There's really only one thing
That can help . . .
And that's me and you.

Mollie Normington (12)
Witton Park Business & Enterprise College, Blackburn

I Have A Dream

The homeless people deserve much more,
It's not their fault they're skint and poor.
They live on the streets all day and night,
Howls and barks give them such a fright.
All they ask for is a bit of dosh,
They've always dreamt of being rich and posh.
Just take this poem into mind,
Spare some change, be really kind.

Tom Butterfield (11)
Witton Park Business & Enterprise College, Blackburn

Freedom In Poems

Poems give you freedom
In every single way,
Just let your mind wander,
Imagination can go a long way.

Please express your feelings,
Your best friends will not laugh,
They just sit and wonder,
With poems, have you chosen the right path?

It's hard to make poems,
But it is really fun,
And if you use your head,
You might be so good you inspire some.

So next time you want to,
Just pick up a good pen,
Write poems about 'owt,
Because I know that you know that you can.

Ashleigh Blades (12)
Witton Park Business & Enterprise College, Blackburn

Eminem

Eminem is his name
He fought for his own fame
First white rapper of all time
He loves spittin' his own rhymes

Brought up in his own town Detroit
Not a good place to be
His childhood was messed up
And no good place to be

Now he is living the high life
In the USA
No one will take that away.

Ben Dodsworth & Crystal Colbert (13)
Witton Park Business & Enterprise College, Blackburn

My Mum Is My Hero

There is only one hero for me,
My hero from my heart I can see.
My hero is my mum.
When I need her she would say 'come'.
There is only one person to turn to,
There is only one person to whom I can say,
'I love you.'
If I had a dream,
She would tell me to work as a team.
My mum would tell me whatever I do,
She is always behind me, so go and have fun.
My mum would say chase your dream and run.
This poem is miles, 100% from my heart,
Nowhere near to a zero.
She is always kind,
She is always on my mind.

Samir Ali (14)
Witton Park Business & Enterprise College, Blackburn

A Bully

If someone calls you a swot,
Then call them a snot . . .
If someone calls you fat,
Then call them a rat . . .
If someone hurts your feelings,
Give them a hard beating . . .
If someone calls you a slag,
Call them a bin bag . . .
If someone calls you poor,
Tell your parents to give them a roar . . .
If someone calls you smelly,
Call them a bully . . .
A bully is always the baby!

Ummehanni Suleman (11)
Witton Park Business & Enterprise College, Blackburn

I Have A Dream

I have a dream that
One day we will have no war.
One day we can look up to the sky
And ask for forgiveness.
The world is changing,
Peace is happening,
People are uniting
And this is happening now.
One day we shall have
One united world.

Ben Eccles (12)
Witton Park Business & Enterprise College, Blackburn

Young Writers Information

We hope you have enjoyed reading this book - and that you will continue to enjoy it in the coming years.

If you like reading and writing poetry drop us a line, or give us a call, and we'll send you a free information pack.

Alternatively if you would like to order further copies of this book or any of our other titles, then please give us a call or log onto our website at www.youngwriters.co.uk

Young Writers Information
Remus House
Coltsfoot Drive
Peterborough
PE2 9JX
(01733) 890066